Flowers by Day, Stars by Night:
Finding Happiness after Loss and Change

By Michelle L. Rusk, Ph.D.

Flowers by Day, Stars by Night: Finding Happiness after Loss and Change

Copyright © 2015 by Michelle L. Rusk

All rights reserved. No portion of this book may be reproduced—mechanically, electronically, or by any other means, including photocopying—without written permission of the publisher.

ISBN: 978-0-9837776-4-9

Library of Congress Control Number: 2015914282

Chellehead Works books are available at special discounts when purchased in bulk for premiums and sales promotions as well as fundraising and educational use.
For details, contact the Special Sales Director at:
info@chelleheadworks.com
505-266-3134
Albuquerque, New Mexico

Printed in the United States of America
First printing September 2015 June 2015

Designed by Megan Mickey
Cover Design by Waya'aisiwa "Gary" Keene
Author Photo by Pamela Joye

Acknowledgements

While I might have written this book, I couldn't have published it without the help of several people. Thank you to Megan Mickey for her always awesome design work. Also, thank you to Sandy, Kelly, Cindi, and MariaElena for their feedback on the content. And thank you to Waya'aisiwa "Gary" Keene for creating the incredible cover of the book. Finally, to my husband Greg who believes in me every day and has made such a difference in my life that my creativity continues to soar like never before.

Strength comes before, during, and after the storm – Waya'aisiwa "Gary" Keene, Acoma Pueblo

Chapter One
Weathering the Storm

On a good day, few of us would open this book. We don't need it when we feel good. When we feel good, when it seems as if life is going our way, we might feel like we can conquer anything. You know, you've been there. Those are the days where we think about all the obstacles that could come our way and we shrug them off. Nah, we think, we can do that. Or we don't believe anything bad will happen to us. It always happens to the people down the street, but not us. And we think of the people who have hurt us, the ones we might not have forgiven and we don't believe they can hurt us again.

This book isn't for those days. There wouldn't be much of a market for that. It's for the days when we can't get out of bed, for when we believe we have been beaten down so much by life that we aren't sure we can even make it through the next hour.

It's about weathering the storm.

The first thing to remember about the storm is that it doesn't last forever. Once when things were so bad in a certain time of my life, a friend reminded me that darkness doesn't last forever. While in the darkness, especially when the sun goes down, everything can feel bleak, but it won't be like that for long. There isn't much hope when the sun isn't shining and we can't see the many steps in front of us.

But sooner or later the sun has to come back out (even if it's a cloudy day there will be light– think how we have to wear sunscreen during the summer even when there are clouds). We might not feel great when light comes back, but we will feel better.

This book is for that darkness when we wonder if the sun, or even the light, will come return. It's for when we can't see in front of us and don't know where to go. And by the end of this book, my hope is you will see that inside you a small ember of a light always burns, even when it's completely dark in your world.

It's hard for the people around us to see us in pain. Our loved ones don't want us to hurt. They also don't want to see us cope with painful situations. And sometimes we have loved ones who aren't supportive (sadly, this is true). For the loved ones who do want to support us, they often pull us toward that light because they want us to see how great our lives are. What they don't realize is that sometimes we just aren't there. We have to acknowledge what hurts so much about why we are coping with whatever it is in our lives. We also need to process it, even for a short time, before we can move into that sunshine.

This book is also for anyone who wants to learn to support someone through a difficult time. To do that, we need to know how to listen and hear someone's pain. We also need to judge less. Ultimately, it's about two things: caring and being human. Supporting someone

Flowers by Day, Stars by Night: Finding Happiness after Loss and Change

we want to be happy means walking in uncomfortable places with them without judging them. Sometimes we go to places others believe we shouldn't because we have to learn something.

While I don't like the lessons that life often presents us, what I do know is that without lessons to learn, there would be no reason to live life. Life isn't perfect and it's not meant to be. We have to weather the storms and the more experience we get, the better we can weather the storm. While it's not always true, generally older people do a better job than younger people. That's because older people have coped with more situations.

Think of this book as your tool kit. My hope is, that by the time you finish reading it, you will have a resource you can return to when you feel yourself slipping into a place you know you don't need to endure. The book always will be available to you to open to the place where you need it. Some chapters will resonate more with certain people than others. And when you get into other life situations, you might find you need different chapters because you have changed. While I encourage you to read it all the way through the first time, use it as a guidebook for future reference.

What you read in here is what I have learned in my life and what I've learned from helping other people. I can't explain how I learned some of these coping mechanism as early as high school. At the time it was simply about motivating myself, but twenty years later I get that I was learning valuable coping skills. And as I've traveled through life, I have repeated mistakes or simply ignored lessons (although I don't believe I did it on purpose so much as maybe I wasn't ready to make those changes).

In recent years I have found myself using these skills when people have reached out to me for help. And it is through these experiences that I realized how I could use what I've learned to help others. I've prayed and asked and left myself open, finally seeing that this is what I'm supposed to do and it's the ultimate way I can help people live the most authentic, meaningful lives possible.

May it do that for you, too.

Chapter 2
Finding Blue Sky

New Mexico is filled with sacred places.

One of my favorites is Acoma Pueblo west of Albuquerque, a mesa where a group of Native Americans built their homes. Today the adobe homes still stand, having been passed down through their families.

For me though, Acoma is as spiritual a place as a church. I have been up there numerous times, taking houseguests for the tour of the mesa. Because they mostly visit in July, which is monsoon season, the day starts out sunny as we drive the ninety minutes west and then south to the pueblo.

Up top, it's hot and dry, the blue sky as clear as far as you can see. The mesa is surrounded by the New Mexico brown dirt, dotted with green cacti and other plants that can survive with a hit or miss rain supply.

But as the day drifts into afternoon, the clouds start to build in the west, just as I see them building from my west-facing backyard in Albuquerque. The clear blue sky suddenly is filled with puffy cotton balls. And then the gray rain clouds. Finally, the lightning and the thunder start their show.

Looking around, standing on what feels like the top of the world yet also in the middle of nowhere, in a place that might have a few satellite dishes and generators, there is still a sense of the primitiveness of life. We are caught up in all that is new and built but being at Acoma strips it down to what life is about: finding peace by connecting to the basic of all aspects of the physical earth around us.

And when the storm rolls in, it's much like life. We start the day in the beautiful sunshine, feeling energized by the newness of the morning. But when the rain comes– and it never lasts long in New Mexico– it can be scary from the intensity of the lightning and thunder. Yet it also cleanses us so that when the sun returns to dry everything out, making it crisp again, we are stronger for it.

We might not like the challenges, the storms that we face, but if we ask what we can learn from them, we'll find that life is much better. We feel hopeful, at peace, and, of course, stronger.

This book is how you find that blue sky again, how hope and happiness are there waiting for you despite everything you've been through. Take it and run with it.

Flowers by Day, Stars by Night: Finding Happiness after Loss and Change

Michelle L. Rusk

Chapter 3
Stars and Flowers

To say I struggled with a title for this book is an understatement. I knew what I wanted: to show that we all can still have great things ahead of us no matter what happens. I used a blue sky theme tentatively and also for a group I ran for separated and divorced women but it didn't feel quite right. I know to "sit" with my book titles and manuscripts, and even the cover designs, but time kept passing by and I had nothing better.

I really wanted to do something with stars and flowers, but nothing came to me. I finally gave up and told myself to just use the blue sky theme.

One weekend in the August before this book was published, I was sitting with my feet in my pool during a weekend party. A friend of my husband's had brought his daughter and she was sitting with me. The four year old held out her little fingers and showed me decals on her nails that I could barely see because her fingers were so small.

"Do you like them?" she asked.

"Yes," I said, adding, "They're Hello Kitty, aren't they?"

"They are," she said, holding up her feet so I could see those, too.

"Stars?" I asked.

"Flowers." She thought for a moment. "But they look like stars."

Finally, from a four year old, my answer.

Several people had brought flowers that day and each time I saw them on the table, I smiled. Flowers and stars. Flowers look like stars.

The next morning I got up earlier than usual, trying to find uninterrupted time to finish this book, and ventured outside to run. It was much darker than my usual time and I instantly looked up and was drawn to the brightness of the Big Dipper in the sky. I hadn't run in that much darkness since spring and I had forgotten how bright the stars are in New Mexico.

While I don't like darkness, I understand that darkness is a necessary part of each day because it's about allowing everything to sleep and start new again. That morning, because I was out much earlier, I enjoyed the sun coming up over the mountains as I continued through my run and then run-walking the dogs. I had such a sense of how important the stars are to us at night.

5

Flowers by Day, Stars by Night: Finding Happiness after Loss and Change

While we must travel through darkness, and because it does take time for the light to rid us of the darkness (if it were that easy this book wouldn't be necessary), the stars are always there, even if clouds cover them. And during the day the flowers are blooming somewhere if not at our homes.

The reminder is that there is always hope no matter what happens to us. We must make the choice to take the journey back to happiness, it's there for us if we choose. And my hope is that because you picked up this book, it's your choice, too.

Chapter 4
Introduction

I never thought that I would write about so much of my life. Growing up, my goal had been to write fiction and that's essentially all I did until my younger sister Denise's death when I wrote my first book about coping with sibling suicide. In each subsequent nonfiction book, I have written about other aspects of my life: becoming a dog person, more about grieving suicide loss, and coping with divorce.

However, this book is a huge departure from past topics because as I traveled through life, particularly the past six years, I began to realize how much I had learned about coping in the years *before* my sister died. I now understand that we often can't see the road– or understand it– when we are on it– and that it's only when we are past it that we can look back, reflect, and at least to some extent get it.

After Denise died, when I was twenty-one and she was seventeen– I thought that part of my life was over, the years that included my sister. And as I worked through my grief I was too focused on understanding why she had ended her life as well as trying to figure out how to go forward with my own life without someone who I thought valued life much more than I did.

But in the years that my marriage unraveled I found that at my core I was still the Michelle I had been before Denise died. While I never thought I would be the same person, like the same things I did before she died, and couldn't believe the gall of someone to say that I would, yes, I still am that person.

And you know what? I really like that Michelle. I'd like to think that I'm a better version, maybe the 4.0 now, but there's a lot about myself that is truly me. I had a road to travel before I could get back to her though.

I don't know that any one of us has the life we expect, but when I reflect back on the journey I've made so far, I never would have thought I'd experience so much loss. At twenty-one my younger sister died by suicide, my maternal grandmother whom I was close to died seven months later, in 2003 my then-husband was hit by a drunk driver and suffered a head injury, my father died in 2006, one of my dogs died of a fast moving cancer in 2008, my marriage ended in 2011, my mother died in 2014. And in that time there also has been the loss of dreams, of friends who have drifted out of my life, and other life happenings that have affected me in some way.

And there has been change. After all, change is also inevitable. If I could, I would cling to the Oven Fresh Bakery on the north side of Chicago, near my maternal grandparents' house and where Mom and I would go after she picked me up from O'Hare on my visits home. It kept me rooted to my childhood. But around the time she died, the bakery also closed. And while I long to taste the perfect kolackys they used to make, the birthday cakes that tasted like birthday cakes should and not what we get at the grocery store, I cling to the memories. And I move forward. I hold that with me, knowing I can't have it back, but also knowing that I can't let it keep me stuck either. I keep the memories even though I let the rest go.

While none of this is unexpected because life is a series of people and events that come and go, I don't reflect back on all that I have lost. Instead, I'm looking at how I've managed to keep my dreams alive despite all that I've been through. There is always much to be grateful for and I have learned the more I'm grateful, the more good that comes my way.

No matter what happened in a day, no matter how badly life seemed, inside of me my dreams continued to burn– and they still do. I always knew that the next day the sun would come over the mountains and it would be like running through the streets of Dingle, Ireland, early in the morning when the pub owners were spraying the sidewalks clean with hoses of water. It was a new day with a clean slate.

But I didn't realize, until I'd experienced multiple significant losses, how many of the skills that I need to go forward and continue to forge the life I wanted were based in what I learned early on: many of the skills I learned in junior high and high school. They were things I taught myself because I knew that I wasn't going to give up on what I'd wanted. Since I was six years old, I knew I wanted to be a writer, an author of books, and that dream has kept me fueled all these years.

Granted, like any dream, it ebbs and flows and sometimes morphs into something else– even if it returns to the original dream– is always there and it's what laid the foundation for everything else.

Chapter 5
Why is all this important to this book?

What you're about to read and learn how to move yourself forward is based on those lessons I learned way back in high school– and to some extent in junior high– when life began to throw lessons at me. I didn't know it then but I managed to teach myself many coping strategies as well as motivating and inspiring myself.

This book is about how I kept that dream alive and how you can do this, too. I won't say it's been the easiest journey I've been on, but I do know when I look back in the rearview mirror I see it's been a road well worth traveling.

While I have added other methods and obviously revised what I learned along the way as the challenges grew bigger, what you're about to use is the crux of what has helped me get where I am despite all the losses and difficulties I have faced.

One final note is that I have written this book to include a spiritual perspective. While not everyone believes in God, to me it's important you believe in some sort of higher power. You have to have a "place" to put things. But for ease of discussing spirituality, I will use God as the higher power in this book. If you have another higher power you believe in, please insert the name there in your mind each time you see God's name.

If you want to get the most of out the book, you'll need to take the time to read it but also reflect on the writings and activities. Sure, you can skip them but when you come to the end and you wonder why you aren't where you want to be, that will be why.

You will probably dislike me at some point while reading this book; you might even throw the book across the room. I don't blame you because there were times I hated the same writings and activities you see here. But when my life didn't progress as I wanted, I realized there was something missing. And that something missing was what I didn't want to do. To be whom you want to be you have to not just revisit, but you need to tackle whatever is holding you back.

You might feel uncomfortable with sections of this book. If you find yourself saying, "Oh, I don't need that." Well, you probably do.

Several years ago I was sitting in the sand at Dog Beach in Huntington Beach, California, after having surfed for a while and I remember the feeling that came over me as I read through a self-help book. I thought those parts didn't pertain to me. Several months later I realized they did, but I wasn't in a space with myself to admit that I needed to delve into those issues. Once I did acknowledge them, a huge piece of my life could move forward, like a plastic game piece on a board game. I was no longer getting the "go back five spaces" cards.

If you find yourself feeling uncomfortable about something, put the book down and write in your journal why you believe you feel that way. Chances are, in your writing you'll start to realize something you didn't want to admit to yourself you did need help with but were afraid to ask.

It's challenging to truly be open to change but by opening that door, bit by bit, you're helping yourself have the best future life possible. It can be uncomfortable in this process and you might question it because of that discomfort. Be assured you are heading in the right direction. If change were so easy, think about how long ago you might have done it. And your next-door neighbor who lives that drama-filled life would have figured out she isn't helping herself by continuing to live in the drama pool.

The key with this book is that you must be honest with yourself. If you don't feel like you can, then put it away for now because you won't find it helpful unless you really want help. Or if you don't want to write about what you're feeling, talk to a trusted friend about it. The hardest part is opening this guide and then starting the journal.

Whatever you do, don't give up. There is no set timeline to get through it nor to making changes in your life, but the more work you do now, the happier you'll be in the long run. It all starts now!

And it's important that you be committed to following through with the activities and journal entries I've included. They aren't in here because I made them up off the top of my head; I've been working with people trying to take their lives forward for more than ten years, I've presented around the world, and I have some idea of what works.

It's also integral that you be willing to work on not just the emotional side of yourself but also your physical, spiritual, and intellectual sides. I never have been open about my spiritual side in the past but I now see that I was nourishing it to some extent all this time; I just didn't call it that.

You will find that by taking care of all four pieces of you, all of which I will talk about more later, that you feel better, feel more hopeful, and see your life moving forward. Think of it this way: if you hurt your foot and you have a hard time walking, somehow you compensate for that which creates an imbalance in your body (usually with the hips) and you find yourself in pain elsewhere in your body. We want to make sure everything is in balance as much as possible so one part of you is not compensating for another. The compensation can't last forever without something else suffering.

I realize that you come to this book at a different point than another person reading it. You might have already done some things. If you have, document those somewhere in your journal and then move on or start where you are. Maybe you've already started an exercise program, then think of it as having a head start on the physical part of moving forward.

By allowing yourself a few vacation days as you work through the book, you're more likely to finish than if you say, "I'm going to do it every day until I'm done" and then when you miss one day, you start to miss another and suddenly you feel as if you have failed. You haven't! Just pick up as soon as you can get back to it. You are allowed to take a "vacation" day occasionally. Maybe you need a day where you want to do something else and that's okay. Again, the key is that you don't let it fester and you pick up the guide where you left off. Think of vacation days as days of rest. Even when you're working at improving yourself, you need to rest a little. And I realize you have family and work obligations.

If you ever feel overwhelmed with pain, sadness, or any other emotion, while you are working in the book then find some positive ways to cope. We will talk about coping mechanisms but right now think of a friend you can talk to or some sort of exercise you can do that will help you relieve those feelings.

During this time, I also suggest you surround yourself with supportive people. There are bound to be people who love and care about you and want the best for you. Allow them to be part of this journey. If they truly do care about you, they will support you as you work your way through it.

If possible, it's always good to find other people who have been through a similar experience. Their stories might not be exactly the same as yours, but you will find as you get to know each other there are many parallels and that what matters most is that you understand each other in a way that other friends and family might struggle to. Share with each other your goals and coping strategies. Be there for each other when you are frustrated or just need to know that you aren't alone in this situation. You will find they are the people who support you the most and you will find you have new lifelong friends in them. While we might cling to each other in times of loss and challenge, it means we also will find hope and happiness and be supportive of each other when good things do happen.

Pace yourself working through the book. Put aside some time when things are quiet and you don't feel hurried. You want to think about what I'm saying and asking you to do. Say a prayer before you read each lesson and ask God to be present with you and help you to be open and learn what you need to learn so you can go forward. Ask God to bring you the responses you need to see clearly how the lesson can help you.

Some of the lessons and thoughts might feel like common sense, but the reality is that most of us forget a lot of the common sense things we should be doing each day, or making part of the routine in our lives. I'm bringing you back to these to learn them where you didn't learn them before or because you don't take the time for them.

This guide is your opportunity to make great changes in your life with long-lasting effects, the kind that will propel you forward to that life, the one you've always dreamed of having. I know that you are standing in a lake of pain right now, one that feels never ending, but believe me when I say it won't last forever. I have watched many people emerge from that same lake and saw what great lives they could still have. Make a choice to start walking out of the lake and onto dry ground where the flowers are blooming and waiting for you. Take it one step at a time and know you aren't alone on the journey.

Know that the feelings are normal. Many others are going through something similar as you. She might even be your neighbor. You don't know what's going on behind closed doors and it's not always what you think. No matter what you believe, you're not alone. And hope is always there.

Every loss we experience has unique aspects to it: losing someone by death is different than divorce. And some will hit us harder than others for a variety of reasons. We aren't going to spend much of our time in this book delving into why you feel the way you do so much as we're going to figure out what it is you need to do to go forward. And find happiness again.

My hope is that by the end of *Flowers by Day, Stars by Night*, you feel like you know yourself better and you know what you want in your future. And you know how to maneuver through the day even when that day isn't necessarily filled with the people and activities that you long for. Yet you feel hopeful the day will come.

Think of me as a coach who is walking alongside of you as you work to take your life forward. I'm cheering you on because I want you to find the hope and happiness that I believe lies beneath the surface in your life. This book is like a guide to get you there. Ultimately you choose the journey and have to walk your life's path, but I'm right there, giving you information, activities, and ideas as you go along.

I've written this book as a way to help others the way I've been able to help myself. It's my gift to you to find not just peace but hope and happiness in your life again. And a future filled with happiness and hope.

As I told a friend once: I am going to catch all the good things in front of me; I'm not going to let them fall to the ground where they'll disappear. Catch all the stars and flowers coming your way.

Chapter 6
Finding Color Again

My kitchen is lime green.

Everyone thought I was making a mistake to paint it such a bold color. But once the white cabinets were installed; the blue, green, and orange tile laid; the gray tile floor put in; and the stainless appliances slid in place, it all came together into something that won a Mohen Faucets remodel contest.

And everyone thought it was brilliant.

But when I moved back to my hometown in the Chicago area after my divorce in 2011, I used white dishes in my kind of blah kitchen. It was a nice kitchen, just needed updating, but I felt as though life there didn't have the color that we do here in Albuquerque and that white would fit better. I thought it was great, like I was making everything simple.

And then I moved back to New Mexico in 2013– a chance to return to my old house (sans the now former husband) with my white dishes in tow.

I hated them.

They felt boring. When taking photos of food for my Chef Chelle food blog everything looked blah to me. I looked around me and the kitchen I still loved and people still raved about. And then I looked outside at how the over 300 days of sunshine made everything look different.

So as soon as I could afford it, I went out and bought new dishes, a set of blue, orange, green, and turquoise Fiesta ware that matched my tile.

It wasn't until later that I realized how much those white dishes reflected such a challenging time in my life. And after I wrote a blog about it, a friend in Luxembourg posted that she had done something similar after the break up with her partner.

While dishes might be a material item, they can be a direct reflection of where we are– and so can other areas of our lives, including the clothes we wear, how much we take care of ourselves, and how much time we spend on ourselves.

No matter what you're going through, I see this as a chance to maybe not reinvent yourself but become who you always wanted to be. I am not diminishing what has ended in your life or who or what you have lost. But the reality is that you can't have the past back. You can't bring a loved one back from the dead nor can you fix a relationship where the other person isn't interested in repair.

But what you can have is a great life no matter what has happened to you. And if you don't believe it, let me believe it for you until you do.

This book is not one where I'm standing in front of you giving you a pep talk and then when it's over, I walk away and you're wondering, what do I do now? This book involves participation by you because only by doing the work will you get to the place you want to be. You can't lay on the couch with ice cream wanting life to be better. You have to make it better.

If you do the work, you will see results much like you do when you start to exercise and eat better. As your body feels better– you have more energy, your clothes fit better– you see the results. You might not see results in the same way from this book, but you will see them in your outlook in life, how you treat people, and how you feel when you wake up in the morning to face the world.

Chapter 7
How did I get here?

I'm sure there is a part of you that despises the idea that you're reading this guide– or that someone asked you to read it because they are concerned about you. You'd much rather be reading that romance novel and lose yourself in someone else's life for a while.

But life has put you here in this spot and although you don't like it, the sooner you accept it, the sooner you will move out of it and onto greater things. When we dreamed about our lives growing up, we all saw what a fairytale we were going to have. Nothing bad would happen to us.

It's not an easy place to be and it's easier to be comfortable in our pain. After all, we believe, why should we think about the future when we have lost something we thought was ours to keep forever?

Most people do not venture out of this place for one reason: they are scared. Fear is what keeps many people from becoming the top of what they should be. We let fear take over because it's, again, easier that way. It's more comfortable to sit with the ice cream and watch movies than it is to get off the couch and interact with the world– or even ourselves.

We forget though that we can still have a great life. Yes, we have lost something that meant a lot to us but that doesn't mean we should give up on it. There is always much more life to live and so much opportunity in front of us. We might not see it because our emotions and our pain cover it up, but it's there waiting to be found.

Slowly, we're going to undercover it in your life, one layer at a time.

Flowers by Day, Stars by Night: Finding Happiness after Loss and Change

Chapter 8
The Commitment

If you want to make this book work for you though, you have to make a commitment. Not to me but to yourself.

As I'm writing, my life has some really great events happening (I was recently married) but I also have had some challenges (a distrustful family member I closed the door on, finally selling a second home I had on the market for two years, and a health issue that required surgery).

While I know that I had to close several doors in my life, I am always confident new doors will open. I could easily lie down on the couch and stay there, but that's not what I want– nor is that really me.

What I want is to move forward. I see this as my chance to continue to carve out the life that I have dreamed of. I have done some carving and as I step away, I can admire the work I have completed. However, I'm not done. We can't do all the carving in one day, but since I want this change to happen, I'm making a commitment to work on the carving daily. And I'm not totally sure that the carving ever will be completely finished.

This book is part of that commitment to myself. I believe that I'm supposed to help others with what I have learned and I know I have done that to some extent. I also realize that if I want to make it happen on a larger scale, I have to take some time each day to work on this guide. It's not helpful to anyone if it remains in my head.

Make a commitment to yourself that you can be the person you want to be. There are days you will want to rest, that's okay, but make sure you make an effort each day, no matter how small, to keep the journey going forward.

Flowers by Day, Stars by Night: Finding Happiness after Loss and Change

Michelle L. Rusk

Chapter 9
A Place To Start

You will need a notebook, something to write in. Find something that reflects you: there are many choices at office supply stores as well as big box stores like Target; a lot of fun styles and patterns. Pick a notebook that makes you happy and think of this as the first step to finding who you are. If you're a crafty person, buy a basic black and white composition book and decorate the cover. With all the fun papers available for scrapbooking, this could be a good project to do to spend some time for you. If you have friends you like to do crafty activities with, you could decorate your notebook during one of those times.

And you might be saying, "What's she thinking? I'm not a writer."

It doesn't matter.

Writer or not, I know writing can be a way to let go of what bothers us and it can be a form of figuring out who we are and what we want just by getting it on paper. Sometimes we find that it changes once we find a place to put it. And it's also a form of prayer, of releasing how we'd like life to be even if we don't sit in a church and ask for it.

I started journaling in sixth grade. It was a requirement for an English class, but after the class was over I had a blank book (I had moved into my brother's room when he moved out and I think he left it behind) and I started to use that to write in. From there I wrote just about every day for years (yes, really!). While often my journal was who I talked to on the phone and what mail I got (yes, really!), when I look back at it, I also see how much I worked out my fears, worries, and frustrations through writing. And it was a place to put my goals and dreams.

It helped me to let go of the stupid things I worried that I said to people or my insecurities as I traveled through my teen years figuring out who I was. It also helped me cope with all the deaths in my life; it was a place where I could say everything I felt without fear of being judged.

Finally, the journals serve as a benchmark of how far we have come. In time, maybe after you finish this book, you'll look back and see how far you've progressed. On a day when you feel like you're taking six steps back, the journal will remind that you that you have come forward and show you how far.

Think of it as motivation for your future.

Before we delve further into the book, let's spend some time in the shallow end of the pool where you're comfortable. We'll get to the deep end shortly. The shallow end is a good place to start though. Later, you can go off the high dive.

Journal

I got my notebook.

Flowers by Day, Stars by Night: Finding Happiness after Loss and Change

Chapter 10
Who are you?

This might be one of the most challenging parts of the books, maybe more challenging than actually making movement forward.

All of our lives have been made up by a variety of events and experiences. I often say that we each bring different colored, shapes, and sizes of luggage with us. I don't say baggage because it's negative and while some events and experiences have been negative, they make up who we are. What we don't have to do is let them define us. Nor do we need to carry them with us. You hate that plaid bag, but you love the purple one? Leave the plaid one behind. Let go of whatever it was that happened to you and stop letting it define who you are today. It's part of you, but does not have to define your life going forward.

In this process called life, sometimes we close the door on who we really are. We might not even know who we are anymore because we are lost in the worlds of others who orbit around us— or who we orbit around. Spouses and children take energy. Parents do, too. And in the daily life of making sure everyone gets off to work and school, of seeing that the dog gets fed, of getting the garbage to the curb, of making sure we do our work to keep the boss happy, we get to the end of the day and realize we haven't done anything for us.

And one day when a loss comes along and yanks away life as we knew it, we realize that we have no idea who we are. And in many ways that can make the loss more challenging to cope with. This is not the time to sit on the couch and drown in Lifetime movies while eating a gallon of ice cream. You only get a short pass on that type of indulgence. This is the opportunity to find out who you are and how to put meaning back into your life so you no longer want to drown in your sadness on the couch. Ice cream is meant to be enjoyed as a treat with others, not the half-gallon carton by yourself.

Earlier, I talked about how I realized many years after my sister's death and a slew of events later how much I was still the same person I'd always been at my core. Then slowly parts of the core of me began to creep into my life. I got a freelance gig writing for my hometown newspaper, the same paper I had won a journalism scholarship from after I graduated from high school.

Then I had an opportunity to take a surfing lesson. I had honestly forgotten how much I had been into thinking surfing was cool. Although living in Illinois it wasn't something I ever had a chance to do nor do I think I would have tried it as a teen— I wasn't that daring. Plus it wasn't something that girls did in the late 1980s. But as I neared forty and a chance opened in front of me, I thought, why not?

I might not be very good at it but now I own a board and I love going to the ocean and having the chance to be out on the water in a way that most people never experience. I understand how you can feel one with the water; I know what it's like to actually ride a wave, catch it, and feel the momentum as I ride the wave to the shore.

In many ways learning to surf changed my life, as if it took me back to where I left off before my sister died and life said, "Hey! Here's the chance you have to be who you always wanted to be!" For me, some of those dreams involve visiting places I've dreamed of (Australia three times) and spending extended time in the Los Angeles area.

I believe that I am my authentic self. While I'm still carving out aspects of my life to truly have the life I want, now more than I ever I believe I am who I am supposed to be. That doesn't mean my life is easy or always happy, but it means when I look around me, I can say, "Yes this is who I am supposed to be."

Reflecting back on my life I can see some of the most important aspects and themes that run through it: writing, running, creating. While running has been a constant through my life, I also realized about five years ago that I was neglecting the fiction writing that had been my dream since I was in first grade when I was creating picture books with stories. Even though I had written two books, one a memoir, one a self-help book, I had put aside something that had always kept me going, my ember of hope.

And so in 2011, I made an effort to finish and publish my first work of fiction, *The Australia Pen Pal*. It made me happy, but as time went on, I realized I wasn't creating as much fiction as I would like.

Cooking, sewing, painting, any sort of creative means, were missing from my life. While writing was always important, it takes a long time to finish something that you can share with the world. Making a meal for others gives me instant gratification in the meantime. However, because of life changes, I wasn't hosting as many dinner parties and it wasn't until I moved back to New Mexico in 2013 that I began to have people over again.

I also took up painting although it was something I hadn't done since Mr. Arlis's Art 3 class in junior high. It gives me another creative outlet and makes me feel like I'm doing what I'm supposed to be doing.

Think back on your life: what kinds of activities have always made you happy or did you enjoy doing? Often we have activities and hobbies we enjoyed but we put them aside to have children, a career, whatever it was. And in that time we got lost as we took care of others.

What did you dream about doing when you were younger? I realize I'm unusual that I knew what I wanted to do from the time I was six years old, that's not the case for most people. However, maybe there was something you wanted to pursue but you weren't able to. It might be too late to make the Olympic swim team, but there are still swimming events where you can compete.

To some extent this is a bucket list, but more it's about what we can accomplish in our daily, weekly, monthly lives. What could we take up that we haven't had time for previously?

Do you have dreams of helping others? There are endless volunteer opportunities no matter where you live. It's easy to find them online, in a newspaper, or ask around. And while it's great to help others, make sure you balance it with doing something for yourself, too. Some people do so much for others that they neglect themselves. We need to have a balance of doing for ourselves and for others in our lives.

And remember that you might try something and realize it's not what you thought it would be or maybe you've changed and you see it's not something you don't like anymore. For instance, I loved the movie "St. Elmo's Fire" and my older sister took a friend and me to see it when we were in junior high (it was R-rated and we couldn't get in otherwise). I thought it was the greatest movie in the world but when I saw it fifteen years later, I didn't like it at all and couldn't finish waching it.

The important part is that you take the time to try activities and to keep trying them. Don't give up after the first time; give it a few more chances. Maybe you just need something a little different than what you've picked. It might be that the yoga studio isn't so close to your house and you find out there is one closer. That doesn't mean you give up on yoga, you just go to the other studio.

Journal:

Who are you?

Don't get scared! This isn't supposed to be a novel. You don't need to write a memoir or your whole life story. Instead, focus on what you believe is important about you. If you had the opportunity to tell someone you had just met about you, what would you want him or her to know? What do you believe would be important for them to know to understand who you are? This could include life happenings (good and bad), your accomplishments, and so forth.

Where you do believe you are stuck?

I know you didn't pick up Flowers by Day, Stars by Night *because you're doing well. Whether you found this book on your own or someone got it for you, it's because something is holding you back. Remember, no one is going to read your journal (unless you choose to let someone see it) so use this as a place to put down what you believe is holding you back. Explain why you believe you're stuck in this particular place.*

Where do you want to be?

This might be one of the hardest questions to answer. You will obviously know you want to be happy again (and knowing that is a huge part of going forward). But what you don't know is how you will get there or what it will look like.

Flowers by Day, Stars by Night: Finding Happiness after Loss and Change

Do you have any idea of what you want your life to look like? What goes through your mind when you think of having a happy life?

What activities and hobbies have you tried in the past? What activities and hobbies do you want to try now?

Be sure to document your experiences, giving yourself space to reflect on them.

Spending time on all these journal entries will help you form a solid base of who you are, where you are today, and where you want to go. Don't worry if you felt like you didn't say enough or couldn't quite answer some of the questions. As long as you got something down, you're doing well.

Chapter 11
Here We Go

While the word disappointment might be an understatement of the pain you feel over your situation, it's an effective way of describing what you feel about something that you thought you would have and suddenly don't.

You might have had visions that you and your spouse were going to sit on the rocking chairs on the front porch for your golden years, reflecting back on your lives with your children and all that you accomplished together. Or maybe you had places you were going to travel to around the world.

Or maybe you had dreams you thought you would accomplish, but then life changed and your loss is realizing that you won't do something you thought you would.

Or possibly a loved one died and you obviously thought you would have more time with that person, no matter who they were to you in your life– a spouse, a partner, a parent, a child, a sibling, a friend.

Whatever has happened to you, there are a million ways to describe it, but it's disappointing that life isn't turning out the way you thought it would. I have often heard that we shouldn't make plans because God laughs at us. While that's true, I also understand what it's like when life changes in ways that are completely unexpected and out of line with how we think they should happen. We believe our marriages will last forever, that our siblings will be with us until we are old, that we will have jobs we like until it's time to retire.

Sadly, it didn't work out that way and you find you're struggling, trying to find your way again as if you are traveling through a neighborhood that has a series of dead-end streets and you can't seem to find your way out of it again. You're cursing the person who designed it while you don't understand how it became this much of a challenge.

Acknowledge your loss. You must start there and no matter how many people are telling you to go on, ignore them for now. Acknowledge what you will never have back again. Write in your journal all that you believe you can't have back.

But remember one thing as you cry your way through the list: a new door will open. While you can't replace the past or have back what was, you still have the opportunity to have a great life ahead of you. You are not closing the door on the memories of what was: those are yours to keep.

What you are closing the door on is the pain that is keeping you from enjoying what is around you, enjoying the people who love you, enjoying, the life that continues. It is hard that life continues– stores still open and close, people still drive to work– while you feel like nothing is the same.

But once you are willing to tell the pain you're done and want to move on, you can throw that key away. There will still be times that it hurts, but as you continue to process through the loss, the waves will subside so that instead of many storms you will be on a tranquil sea where you can see the sea life and sand of the ocean floor in the water below you.

This is not about time either. There is no set time that what's ahead will be the same for everyone. Everyone experiences loss at different levels. Don't compare yourself to anyone else, this is your journey.

Take the time to process this. Let the sadness wash over you and know that each time you do that, you are letting go of the power it has over you. Eventually that will dissipate as well.

The hope is also that by letting go of the bad memories and the anger at how things turned out, you will be able to forgive and remember the good things. There is no sense in getting caught up in only thinking about the bad (and we will talk more about how to cope later). If you truly want to go forward, you will need to force yourself to let the bad go, no matter how comfortable it may be to hang onto it.

There is work ahead of you but you can do this. We're all walking this road together.

Journal

What do you believe you can't have back in your life?

Chapter 12
Reflecting on the Past

This is the only opportunity I will give you to reflect on the past. While the past is important because it has helped define who you are (although it doesn't define you– it's just a piece of that puzzle that makes up the whole you), it's important because some of what happened in the past is why you're reading this book.

I didn't write this book as a way for you to bash people in your past for how they hurt you. Instead, it's about pulling out the shoebox that you've written in marker "The Past" on the side and opening it up. You're going to take out all the pieces of the past and turn them around and examine them as if you have never seen them before.

Why? Because you need to take a step back from these experiences and stop letting them hurt you. You're wasting your energy and many people use them as excuses to keep from moving forward in life.

It doesn't have to be that way. No one has to keep the past from hurting them. I'm not saying that one day you'll be able to get up and say, "The past will never hurt me again" and it won't. That's not realistic. However, you can learn to manage the hurts from the past and use them to go forward rather than keeping you stuck there.

Take some time, probably over a few days, to think about the life experiences that are hurting you the most. There are probably one or two that led you to this book in the first place. However, as you start to delve into your life, I'm sure you will come up with some others that, while you knew they were there, you didn't realize how much they were hurting you.

Spend time writing about them. What happened? Who are you angry at? Why? Are you angry with yourself? Why?

And then ask yourself, why do you keep letting these people/events hurt you?

Usually the other person involved in our situations doesn't care (or presents it like they don't care to keep themselves from hurting more). While it might not be right that they don't have any feeling about it, we can't control others. What we can control our own emotions.

Bottom line: the past isn't worth dwelling over. That part has already been written. Now it's time to work on writing the future you want.

Journal

What life experiences are hurting you the most and keeping you from moving forward?

Flowers by Day, Stars by Night: Finding Happiness after Loss and Change

Chapter 13
The Journey

It's easy to think, "Okay, if I can just get past this, all will be well."

What we don't realize is that it's about the road we take to get past our pain.

When I finished my master's degree in 1996, a high school friend sent me a card that talked about how it was about the journey, not the destination. It was the first time that it hit home to me how life is a process.

I always have been a person who is about the destination. In my mind I have constantly imagined what life would be like when I accomplished each of my goals. And while this was positive, it only was good for me to some extent.

When I embarked on my doctorate, a man I substitute taught for often at the high school where I coached— he also had a doctorate— quickly reminded me to slow down when I said I wasn't interested in the coursework, that I just wanted to get to the doctorate.

He recommended I read the book *Seabiscuit* about the racehorse that defied odds. I didn't realize it at the time, but as I traveled through my coursework I began to understand what he was talking about. The courses led me to places I wouldn't have discovered on my own: learning about family systems led to my book *Rocky Roads: The Journey of Families through Suicide Grief*. Additionally, in those classes I also was given opportunities to explore further the relationship between dogs and their human companions with the end result: my dissertation about how people use dogs to help them cope with human loss.

It's easy to look at life and think about how each step of the way is about the destination, but it's more than that. Through our life experiences, we learn more about how we handle circumstances. We also learn how strong we are. I equate it to running a race. If we just jog it, yes, it's easy but there is nothing rewarding from it. If we push ourselves, we learn how strong we are, that we can reach down deeper inside ourselves than we would have thought otherwise possible.

And when a situation happens to us— like a loss— those are the opportunities to pull from it the strength that we didn't realize was there. We could walk the race and continue to be miserable and sad, but if we reach inside and work at it, once we cross the finish line, we will look back and see, "Wow, I had no idea I could do that."

After all, we must journey through the past to get to the future.

Journal

Write about one major loss in your life and what you learned from it.

Activity

Light a candle and say a prayer asking that you let the past go so you can allow the brightest future possible to flow into your life. Spend a few minutes letting this sink in and listening for God to speak to you. If you don't hear anything, it's okay. We will work on this as we go forward in the book.

Chapter 14
Fear

Fear is a double-edged sword. There are good aspects to it but there also are pieces of it that can cause us to act in ways that we never thought we would. Mostly fear is something we allow to control us when we shouldn't.

On the positive side, fear can bring us added energy that can be helpful. We perform better when we have an element of fear inside ourselves. As long as it's not overwhelming and it's just enough to heighten our senses and our need to do well. We are nervous because we don't know the outcome but we know that if we do our best, we can let go of what it will look like in the end.

But there is also fear of the unknown that we allow to control us and that's the fear that can lead us into places we never thought we'd go. For many people, it's the fear of the unknown, which also can be the fear of being alone.

If we have been in a relationship before and it ends (especially a long one) or you believe the fact that you're getting older and you're still not married means you will never find someone, you might find yourself entering relationships that you would never take on before.

These can be the unhealthiest relationships because they are insecure and the other person usually knows how insecure you are and will take advantage of this. People often enter into sexual relationships during this time, worrying they will never have sex again and that fear leads them to want it all the time. The insecurity breeds a feeling that isn't real and the person continues tolerating being treated badly by the other person because she starts to think that this is all there is for her. She tolerates it because she has lost hope that there is something better and she will tolerate all the complicated messiness of a relationship that really isn't a relationship because of her fear of being alone.

Or someone won't enter a relationship at all because she's afraid that she will get hurt again. Instead, she builds a wall around herself and keeps anyone interested from penetrating that wall. She would prefer to be lonely than allow herself to be vulnerable and experience love.

Think of fear like wine: for most of us one glass is enough. We realize our limits and we enjoy that glass. Fear is the same: having some fear makes us perform better. But when we start to drink too much we often do things we usually wouldn't do. So having too much fear makes us act in ways that later when we look back, we think, "That was me? Why did I do that? I never would have done that."

Flowers by Day, Stars by Night: Finding Happiness after Loss and Change

Making fear disappear is a challenge but it's one that can be overcome with security in ourselves and who we are.

Turn fear into faith. When you get caught up in fear, think about what you want in life and how you're going to get there. Stay in the present where neither the past nor the future can hurt you. Be at peace where you are. As you travel through this book, you'll learn more ways to cope and how to spin your perspective into one that's more positive.

You've developed some other behaviors in your life that need some undoing– we all have– like knots. Remember, the behaviors all stem from fear and once we look fear in the eye, the knots will loosen and we can undo them.

Fear is passing. Fear is not constant. Remember that if you feel afraid, you can't be fearful forever. It's like the sun always comes up.

Journal

What do you fear and how can you change it?

Chapter 15
Making the Choice

No one can make the choice to move forward but you. As I mentioned at the beginning of the book, there are going to be times when you won't like me and this might be one of them.

Everyone one of us has choices to let go of the past and to get off the couch and stop feeling sorry for ourselves. I realize it's much easier to stay on the couch, after all, getting up means putting energy into something and when we feel hopeless, depressed, and drained.

But if you stay on the couch you're missing out on life. There's a whole world outside your window, outside your front door, but if you stay inside the world is not going to come to you. You need to get up and make the first step and that first step is choosing to go forward.

I will never say any of this is easy but I do know that it's worth it. So get up, with the book in hand, walk outside, and look around you. (I'll add a note here that I understand if the weather is bad and you don't want to go outside, but try to do this exercise when the weather gets better.)

Do you hear the birds singing? Is the sun shining and warming you? Is everything green? Take a moment to just be in the moment. Is the sun bouncing off the snow? Can you see the raindrops splashing the on asphalt?

This is what you want– to feel everything around you that has hope in it. After all, how can you not feel hopeful when the birds are singing every morning?

You still must make that choice though. Some days you say "forget it" and think it's better to roll over and stay in bed, but those are the days when you need to get up and get moving. Don't lie around all day in your workout clothes. You'll feel lazy, like a blob, and it will feed the emotions that you don't need to get up and do anything. Get out of bed and do something that makes you happy.

When you've made the choice to shed the past, to shut doors that you've been leaving open, you'll see your life start to change. It might not be obvious at first, but it'll happen.

Journal

What happened when you walked out the front door?

Flowers by Day, Stars by Night: Finding Happiness after Loss and Change

Chapter 16
The Parallel Journey

While you are processing what you have lost, you also will take the journey of finding not just peace, but hope and happiness again. For a while, these two roads will travel together, such as how in some places the interstates were laid next to the old Route 66. Sometimes you can see it when you are on the interstate– the frontage road that travels right next to it. And in other places you don't know where Route 66 was because the interstate was placed directly on top of it.

When you begin this journey, you will feel some days as if you aren't moving forward at all, like you are stuck in one place. But other days you will sense that you're traveling on both journeys as you work to let go of the pain and hurt of the past and look forward to what's ahead.

As this happens, you'll notice that as you process what you have lost and begin to shed it, you don't always see the road parallel to you. You might only see the interstate. That's because your journey will eventually become one about taking your life forward. You won't ever completely let go of the past– the goal is to remember the good times and what you've learned, but the road won't be so obvious anymore.

Flowers by Day, Stars by Night: Finding Happiness after Loss and Change

Chapter 17
Never Say Never

You believe you will never love again. It doesn't matter if it's a romantic relationship or your family. You tell everyone to stay clear, that you're done, that you won't let anyone near you again.

Of course you feel this way. You're in a lot of pain and this is a typical feeling.

However, it's not the way you really feel. You only feel this way because you want to protect yourself from any hurt. But life is about being connected to others and at some point as you continue to move your life forward; you will find yourself not wanting to be alone.

Don't let your current feelings cloud how you truly feel. Know that the hurt you feel now won't last as long as you do work at making this an opportunity to forge ahead and be who you're supposed to truly be.

Flowers by Day, Stars by Night: Finding Happiness after Loss and Change

Chapter 18
The Patience Game

I won't say that I am the most patient person in the world. To hear someone say "patience is a virtue" does not fit me at all. Having a cell phone that does everything for me but cook dinner has made it worse. I find myself more irritable at red lights and in the grocery store when I have to wait. Looking at my phone passes the time, yet when I don't have access to them, there is nothing to check, or the network is too full to let me do anything, I start tapping my foot and feel antsy.

It hasn't been much different in my life. Quite honestly (and I'm being serious about this!), I thought many things would happen to me by the time I turned twenty-three. That's many good things. I had grand plans and I saw no reason why they wouldn't happen by then. These dreams were shattered long before my sister died and altered other dreams. I don't believe I thought life ended at twenty-three, I just thought I was bound for great things early.

As I continued to travel through life, I still thought certain aspects should move faster, particularly the success of my writing career. Why wasn't I selling more books? Why didn't I have an agent? It was difficult when people would ask me constantly about these things or tell me how great my work and story were and that I should be on Oprah.

That wasn't meant to be either. Or was it?

While I admit there are some days where I struggle, thinking about what I believe should have already happened or I look at my nine published books, the workshops I have created that I have never been able to sell to people, and I wonder why I can't reach more people. Isn't the object of this to reach as many people as possible?

Patience, people said.

What I had to accept is that each piece I create– a talk, a book, or something else, is all part of the journey. And it's one that I not only have to be patient with, but also I have to trust and have faith in (which we will address soon). When I do something, I'm putting together another piece of what is to come. On a good day, one where I don't feel frustrated or stagnant, I get it. I can see the road behind me and how the puzzle pieces are coming together. But on a day when I sit in my office and wonder why I'm not reaching more people or making a better living, I feel like I'm in the grocery store and left my phone on the dining room table.

Much of what we learn about patience comes from life experience. I know that all of us are more patient now than we were as high school teens, when we thought we understood everything only to realize how little we really did until we moved into the reality of the real world, beyond the cocoons of our families.

Patience also comes to us from activities. Running taught me that I could improve and be better at anything I wanted to do. While I was frustrated at the four years to earn my bachelor's degree, I knew there was a means to the end and I had to continually remind myself that each piece, even those awful math classes, were part of the larger picture to get me past the degree that I knew was part of getting me into the world where I wanted to be.

Those aren't the only ways I have learned patience though. I grew up being terrible at anything relating to a ball. I could use a million excuses— my eyes don't work together, my older sister said I was never interested in throwing a ball around— but that doesn't mean it had to be that way. I see now that I just wasn't patient. It didn't come naturally to me so that meant I would have to work extra hard at it. I never did.

However, when I invested that kind of time and effort into running, my patience did pay off. I got better and better and felt like the possibilities were endless. Now that I have taken up several sports: surfing plus two that involve balls— tennis and golf— I am much more relaxed with myself. I can't always hit the ball, I don't always catch a wave. However, I am willing to keep trying because I know that the more I try, the more patient I am with myself, the better I will become.

While it might seem counterproductive, the reality is that slowing down actually helps us to move forward quicker. It's not about relaxing the pace so much as relaxing us. The patience game pays off in the end if we choose to play.

Journal

What has taught you patience? Where do you need to do a better job with it?

Chapter 19
Self Talk

It's all about how you talk to yourself. I remember back in my junior high and high school running days the quote "If you think you're beaten, you are." While we weren't born to think badly of ourselves, as we have encountered people in our lives in some ways they might have beaten us down to the point where we aren't secure and we think others are better than us. It may have started at home with our families or maybe it was kids at school who made fun of us.

Often we get caught up in all the things we don't like about ourselves. We look in the mirror and we don't think, "I have great hair!" Instead we focus on our nose and how much we wish it were smaller or maybe not so fat. We do the same with our bodies, with our personalities, our outfits, anything about us. No matter how great we look to other people, we think we look terrible to ourselves.

Life has created this. Think back on all the times you were made fun of growing up. Or about the time you thought you had this great outfit and one day at school someone made fun of it and you never wore it again. And the day a boy you liked made fun of your nose? You never saw it the same way again.

These situations have left you not liking yourself and because the kids made fun of your nose or the fact that you wear glasses, even years later you still look in the mirror and wish you could be someone else.

Stop right there.

You aren't beaten and you need to stop thinking that you're beaten.

Now you're going to think about what you *like* about yourself. And from now on this will be your focus. That nose is just fine and I'm sure someone else told you how much he or she liked it, but you dismissed it because you were so used to hating it.

The language that we speak to ourselves has the same effect as we let others have on us with what they say to us. It's true that if you see the glass half full, life is brighter and has more to offer. Think about some of the phrases you say to yourself and then look at how you can turn them around if they are negative.

"I'll never finish school."

Turn it into,

"I will finish school."

Or

"Nothing good ever happens to me."

Make it,

"Lots of good things happen to me."

Do not accept any negativity from yourself and if someone says something negative to you, immediately turn it into something positive in your mind. Like everything in this book, it will take time to change, but you can change. The more positive you are, not only do you feel better, but you'll see you attract happier and more productive people around you. And you'll start to feel more confident, like you can take on the world.

That's the you you want to see because we all should feel that way. Hold your head high and be grateful for every part of you. I could list a million parts of me that I don't like, but I have learned those make up me and if I take time to focus on them, it's not helping me be productive. I talk to myself in a positive manner because then the glass feels like it's not just half full, but bubbling over.

This doesn't mean my head won't fit into the front door of my house because my ego is so big. It means that I am proud of who I am and what I offer not just myself but also the world around me.

No matter what has happened to you, you're still a worthy person and you deserve not just a peaceful life. but a happy one filled with joy and laughter. However, if I ask you what you like about yourself I bet you would look at me with a blank face. Take some time— over a few days— to complete the journal exercise below.

Journal

Title a page in your journal "What I like about myself" and the first thing I want you to write is what you dislike most about yourself. This is where you need to begin: by making peace with yourself. Then keep listing what you don't like about yourself.

When you're done with the list, start on what you do like about yourself. Begin this list at the top as another column. I'm sure the column of what you actually don't like about yourself is longer than the like.

Look over the list and tell yourself how much you like everything you've written about yourself. Turn your thoughts around about what you don't like. Instead of " I hate my nose" turn it into "I have a very cute nose."

I'm guessing by the time you're done you'll be giggling at yourself. Whenever you catch yourself saying you don't like something about yourself— especially in the bathroom mirror— force yourself to turn it around before you walk away or think another thought.

By liking yourself more, you'll find you're actually happier as you interact with the world. You will find you want to take care of yourself because you appreciate more what you have.

Like everything else in this book, these changes will not happen overnight, but they will happen if you take the time to work on them.

You're worth it, right?

Flowers by Day, Stars by Night: Finding Happiness after Loss and Change

Chapter 20
Letting Go

I see writing a book like molding a piece of clay.

While I have many manuscripts I have started and not finished, mostly I do want to finish them but it's hard for me to focus on one thing partly because I have a lot going on and then I get excited about working on something else. But this manuscript has been one of the hardest to see the true vision of what it's supposed to be. I have started and stopped this manuscript more times than any previous one.

I have multiple saved copies of what I thought this book was supposed to be. I have written some of the same pieces repeatedly. Finally, I had to ask God for some help. "Show me what I'm supposed to write," I prayed repeatedly.

I kind of hoped a sticky note would drop from the sky and show me what that is but I know that God isn't always that obvious. I had to be more open to listening.

Each week when I went to my group for separated and divorced women, we continually came back to the same challenge: letting go. Finally, one of the women looked at me and said, with a lot of passion as she raised her arms, "But how do we do it?"

I knew what she meant. Letting go has never been my forte and it's a lesson I am continually faced with. I am much better about it now but it's been a long road for me to get here and I can see the lessons thrown at me over the years as I reflect back.

I always talk about how some of the biggest lessons life taught me came from running track and cross-country. However, I did a terrible job learning this lesson during my years of running competitively. There were many other aspects of life I learned well during that time but this wasn't one of them. I held onto hurts and worries too tight.

It wasn't until my sister's death that I was forced through the ultimate letting go: the death of a loved one. It was the lessons I had learned before that, because she died just three years after I graduated from high school, things like how to keep going on a long run, which is much like how to survive grief, put me in a better place than I might have been otherwise. Losing Denise forced me to learn it in a most unpleasant way, much the way difficult lessons in our lives come to us.

Through the years I have continually been faced with letting go, especially through the losses of people I cared about. But I have also had to let go of situations in my life that were keeping me from moving forward, like my now former marriage.

But each time I've let go, I've moved forward in my life. I've stepped out of my box and had new experiences come to me. It's not been easy but I've kept myself open to what life could hold. I've kept the glass half full even when I've been in so much mental pain that I wondered what it was all worth. There was always a light burning somewhere inside of me.

After she asked that question in the group that night, I realized that's what I needed do. If letting go had been so hard for me and I had learned so much from it, then it was time for me to share how I did it. We all have the opportunity for the best life possible. By letting go, it's a huge step forward.

There are multiple ways we must let go to move forward. Don't fear this because letting go always means there is something better for you. Remember, always when one door closes another opens. It might not happen right away, but believe. It will happen.

I think of the example a priest I know used with me several years ago. He had talked about how sometimes we are asked to give up things or people in our lives. This is very painful but he reminded us that it's because God has something better for us.

When he said this, because of my divorce, I had given up my remodeled house with the pool in Albuquerque that I loved and two of the four dogs to move to my hometown in the Midwest to a house I liked but not nearly as much as the one in Albuquerque. I had worked hard over a period of years to turn the Albuquerque house into something I love. A friend asked, "But how can you give up all your furniture?" knowing all the time I had spent collecting a slew of mid-century items, redoing them, and placing them perfectly in the house.

"That means I'll have better furniture one day," I said, holding onto the prospect of a happier future. After all, it was just furniture. It was replaceable. It wasn't worth continuing the relationship over furniture.

But when I had the chance to move back, I felt as if I were the country song joke when people ask, "What happens when you play a country song backward? You get your house back, your dog back…" That's exactly what happened to me.

So when Fr. Anthony brought this up, I said, "I gave up the pool once, I'm not doing it again."

He thought for a moment and finally asked me, "What if God asked you to give up your pool for, say, the ocean?"

It made sense. When we give something up– often not because we want to– it's because God has something better in store for us.

The most frustrating part is that we don't know what that "something better" is and we never know when it will come along. But we must be patient, believe, have faith, and continue to travel on our journey in the mean time.

We also hold on tight to whatever it is we need to let go. The idea of letting go of a loved one who has died is not only painful but also very scary. But it's not what you think it is: the memories are yours and you won't lose those by letting go. No one can take the history of what you shared with that person. And that loved one is still part of your life, although not in the same way. Instead, what you're letting go of them in your future as they were in your past. It won't be the same but they are still in your life, they are still with you, and it takes time to get used to the idea that it's different.

If it's the end of a relationship, again, you still share the memories of that person. You need to move on because there is no turning back– that person doesn't want to be with you. By holding on, all you're doing is hurting yourself. He doesn't care– whether he has truly moved on or not is irrelevant because this is about you and the great life you have ahead of you.

Finally, we must let go of outcomes. None of us knows what the future holds and by thinking too much about it, we end up depressed. I have found myself in the past wanting to know so badly what the future would bring and what I finally realized was that I needed to be happy in the present because thinking too much about the future was starting to hurt me. And we can't live in the past because we can't change it. We must keep ourselves rooted in the here and now, right where our feet are planted. When we do that, we'll find we feel more peace. And happiness.

And it's like we're throwing a boomerang.

We all know what a boomerang is: it's an object that looks like an arrow or the letter V that is thrown and because of its shape it will bounce back at us. I also think of it as a "come back here" because it does come right back.

What we are doing with our losses and challenges is throwing them out like a boomerang. We might write what we need to let go of on the boomerang or we just know that the boomerang is a symbol of the challenge.

However, we must be prepared for when the boomerang returns, it might not look like it did when we threw it.

When I think of this, I am standing outside and I throw my boomerang. What I don't realize is there is Jesus standing in the distance in his white robes and rope sandals and he catches my boomerang. But he doesn't let it come back to me nor does he even talk to me about returning the boomerang.

I get so frustrated that I sit on a low stonewall and wait. And Jesus is patient; he's holding onto my boomerang, it's tucked under his arm, while I sit.

I have learned some big lessons in giving up what I have for something bigger. Now some things we can't control letting go of because they are taken away from us. Others we hold onto, even when the other person is long gone emotionally or a situation has ended. What we don't realize, because we are too wrapped up in our pain, is that we are keeping ourselves from receiving something bigger.

It's a challenge to let go of something, even when we know we should. But it's the unknown that scares us.

And it made sense. While we might be giving up something we really care about, or believe is ours, we must trust that there is something greater for us out there. By keeping doors open, by holding onto hope of something that will never be, we are keeping the boomerang from coming back to us. Although when the boomerang comes back, it won't look the same, it will actually be a nicer one, even better than what we could have imagined.

So while we are hurt because we must give up someone or something we thought was so important in our lives, one day the answers will reveal themselves and we will look back and understand.

Journal

What are you being asked to give up in your life? Has this happened to you before? Reflect on what you received in return. Remember, it might not be as obvious as you think; you might need to reflect over a period of time.

Chapter 21
The Unknown

After my marriage ended and I started working with a Catholic priest on an annulment, I also met with him periodically to check in. It was a good way to keep me balanced. I have a tendency to get stuck in my head and he could help me see that my thoughts weren't reality.

(I am putting a disclaimer to the next statement: I am a dog person and I don't mind cats: what I say below is a stereotype and just that, nothing more.)

One day I sat in Fr. Josh's office and I told him something that had been bothering me.

"I'm worried that I'm going to end up like one of those women who lives alone with her cats."

He didn't respond at first, as if he were waiting for me. And then I realized why. It was ridiculous. "That's not going to happen, is it?" I asked, knowing that hearing it out loud had a different effect.

"No," he said, shaking his head.

It's a very real and scary feeling for anyone who has been through the end of a relationship, especially a marriage. We thought we had a partner for life. While we complain about the routine of life, we do know that having someone to share it with does make a difference. We can be on our own and experience life independently, but having someone to travel the road of life with makes it more fun.

We worry that we won't have someone to love us again. We think that we're destined to be alone. There are a million reasons we think that and it's not helpful, no matter how much people tell us we will find love again, to hear it. So often I wanted to scream at people, "You have someone! You aren't alone! You aren't walking in my shoes!"

We don't want to be desperate, but there is a desperation about us because of our fear. I found myself reaching out for astrological readings. I wanted to know my future; I wanted to know who was in my future. I didn't get the answers I wanted (especially because the astrologist I used is very New York blunt and doesn't tell you what you want to hear so much as what you need to hear).

This experience is going to take us to the depths our pain, a place we feel like we have already been too many times before. It's a place that I wish I could wave a magic wand and see the pain go away from all the people I see struggling.

No one can make our pain go away though. We have to travel through it and the key is that we have to trust and have faith about the journey. For me, it was as if intellectually I understood it: I would have love again when it was time. But for my heart, it hurt that I was alone especially because I lived in a very family centric town and at church everyone seemed to have someone. Except me.

While some people feel that their kids are a burden in marriage break ups, the reality is that for many more their kids keep them going and keep them connected. I didn't have children and I had to do it on my own in a place where everyone else seemed to have what I didn't. I tried to remember that life isn't perfect when the front door is shut and locked for the night, but it didn't always help. What I saw was painful enough.

I taught myself to be okay with the unknown and that's how the pain finally subsided.

Journal

What do you feel is unknown in your life?

Chapter 22
An Ember of Hope

In the winter here in New Mexico we can see the city lights better because there are no leaves on the trees. This leaves holes in what normally would be full vegetation. From my upstairs window there is a spot between the houses above the rooftops where I can spot just a glimmer of the city lights at the base of the Sandia Mountains.

And when I'm out run-walking my dogs Chaco and Hattie in the morning, there is a spot where we turn to come back to the park just a few blocks from our house and there is just enough of an incline that I can see the city lights up north.

While these aren't necessarily the most obvious places one would see city lights– not quite as easily viewed as when one comes over a hill on Interstate 40, driving back into Albuquerque, and suddenly the city comes into complete view, a panoramic view that seems endless, with continuous glittering lights– they are reminders that the city lights are always there.

There are days we feel as if our life is filled with hope and happiness like the endless lights, but often after times of loss and change, we can feel like everything is dark.

But it's not.

Somewhere inside of each of us an ember of hope burns. We might think it's not there, we might even deny it's there because we are so angry and hurt about what has happened to us, but it is. It's that very ember that has kept me going through the times of loss and change in my life.

And when I see these small pockets of light, I think the embers must look like them. They might not be easy to see, sometimes we have to know where to look, and they might only last for a short time because when we move a step or two, they are gone.

They are there though.

Journal

What are your embers of hope? What blocks you from seeing your embers of hope? What keeps them lit for you?

Flowers by Day, Stars by Night: Finding Happiness after Loss and Change

Chapter 23
Being Present

I admit to being a daydreamer. I was the kid who sat in class and used to look out the window and wonder what the rest of the world was doing in the morning while I was there in school. I had good grades, but many times I was lost in thinking about the life I dreamed of or relationships I would have with boys. Or the boy I thought who would make my life better.

I spent so much time thinking about my future that I wasn't as present as I should have been in my life and I missed out on quite a bit.

If we spend our time thinking about the past, on what we are hurt about or what we miss, the present will pass by us and we won't realize it until it's gone. We can't DVR life like we can our favorite television shows. We can't forward through what we don't like nor can we rewind what we missed.

And if we are too caught up in the future, we will miss the present, too, because we're too busy thinking about what we want to have, not where we're standing right now.

But if we are in the present, right here, right now, where life has us, there won't be any regrets. Sometimes after someone leaves our lives— whether because they have died or because they don't want to be with us— we start to think "If only…if only I had been available then. If only I had been listening and not too busy reading a magazine. If only I had taken the time…"

There is no "if only" if we are present.

And if we quit thinking about where we were and where we want to go, there is peace in that. Take a moment to sit right where you are. Close your eyes if you need to and just rest. Be in the moment. Enjoy what and who is around you.

Yes, you can enjoy memories from the past and you can plan for the future, but you need to be right where life has you so you don't miss out.

Journal

Where are you present in your life? Where can you do a better job being present in your life?

Flowers by Day, Stars by Night: Finding Happiness after Loss and Change

Chapter 24
Rituals

Letting go and trusting aren't easy (and I'm guessing some people are snorting as they read that line). It's a cinch for anyone to say, "You need to let go of him. You need to move on." But then they don't offer any words of advice of *how* to go about that. Much of life is about letting go because it's ultimately about trusting and having faith. That all goes back to the fear of the unknown.

We've all been told at some point that if we let a door close, another will open. As we travel the letting go journey, keep that at the back of your mind. Letting go means that you are closing a door and you are having faith that another one will open although you don't know how that will play out.

There are different ways we can tell ourselves to let go but for many of us, having a ritual to do, a physical act of doing something, is what works best. There are many rituals that one can perform and we'll talk about a few ideas here.

The first one is lighting a candle. The flame in a candle represents something significant in our lives. For some of us, it's simply the idea that the flame is light and helps us to see the light. For others of us, flames are related to sacred spaces and religious or spiritual settings.

Whatever the reason, lighting a candle is a good ritual for letting go. I sometimes will light a candle— at church, other times at home before I go to bed, but most likely first thing in the morning when I sit down at my desk to work. I'll spend five minutes in prayer, part of it asking for help, part of it listening. If I do it at church, I say a prayer with it and then leave the candle lit at church. At home, I will say the prayer and then blow out the candle when I'm done. Both ways are helpful to me but some people might find leaving a candle lit works better than blowing it out or vice versa.

Sometimes touching something (I use a rosary) and repeating a mantra or phrase can work. For me, the rosary worked because I would touch each bead and repeat something like "I am moving forward" until my anxiety dissipated.

Another ritual is to do a burning. Write a letter to the person who has left your life. This letter can be whatever you want it to be. You can write about your anger or any other feelings you have at the time. You can talk about the life events you're sad not to be sharing with that person or other aspects of your life that aren't the same and you find painful because they aren't part of them now.

Flowers by Day, Stars by Night: Finding Happiness after Loss and Change

Or you can write the letter as a goodbye to the past, that you know it's time to go on and how you will be not just be fine but be great. And how thank you are for the time you had together but you realize sometimes people aren't meant to spend their lives together. You might not believe this, but in time my hope is that eventually you will be able to look back and smile on the past and where your life is headed. Whatever you had isn't anymore and there is no reason to dwell on it.

When I had a relationship end, my neighbor, whom I called the Greek God because he loved women, said to me, "Did you enjoy your time with him? I always look back and remember the good times."

He was right.

While it takes processing to get to that point, writing the letter is a step in that direction because it's something you can complete. You might not be able to talk to the person for a variety of reasons, but writing the letter is an action-oriented activity that you can do.

The other piece of this is to make a list of everything you want to do. This is what might be tricky for some of you who have squashed your list so far down under everything else in your life.

While this isn't necessarily the 50 goals list you'll do later in the book, it's most of a list of who you want to be. Do you want a new partner in your life? Do you want to live somewhere else? Have a different career? Do you want the pain to go away so you can be happy?

Whatever it is, this is the place to put it.

When you've written all you want, have a burning of the letter/lists. You might even do this with a few others. The women in my group and I did this several times with my Weber grill. My mom had just died when we did the first one and my house was filled with palms from various Palm Sundays. The appropriate way to dispose of these is to burn them (they actually make up the ashes we Catholics receive on Ash Wednesday) and Mom had collected them over several years, refusing to do anything with them but burn them yet she never did that so she had amassed quite a collection.

The women and I gathered around the lit grill and I threw the palms in and then each one tossed her letters on top. Mine was a list and it went last. As we watched them burn, we said a few prayers, cracked a few jokes, and took some time to be together as we worked to shed the past. We did this again at the end of the year as a way to close out the old and bring in the new.

Burning is symbolic to me because it's a way of releasing whatever it is that hurts you and you want gone from your life or a way to throw out to the universe what you do want.

Once, before my mom and I moved to Albuquerque, she was in the backyard burning a stack of bills. I think she was too frustrated with her shredder and decided to burn them

Michelle L. Rusk

instead. I was annoyed with someone in particular in my life; feeling like things weren't where I wanted them to be. I wrote, "Help!" on a sticky note and threw it in her fire on top of her papers.

In many ways it was an SOS. While I know that God is with me, sometimes I still struggle and feel alone and I was asking for some immediate help.

Burning is a cleansing and taking the time to do this, alone or with others, is yet another step taking you forward. You might find you need to do it a few months later and that's okay, too. Or do it on your birthday, on an anniversary, at the end of the year, on any day that is significant to you.

There are many other rituals that someone can do. The point is that they be meaningful to you. You might find that it's something you need to do repeatedly before you feel any movement forward. That's okay. Nothing will change overnight. It's like we are relearning (or learning for the first time) how to cope with life. And the more we perform the ritual, the better it will serve us in the future.

Rituals are also a way of distracting ourselves. We use them to take the immediate pain away. While they are important to add as a routine into our lives, they also can be used in the moments when we feel pain and anxiety and we don't know what to do with it. At those times, it's best to perform a ritual than do something you might regret later (drinking a bottle of wine, eating that half gallon of chocolate ice cream, spending too much money on clothes– you get the idea).

The need for the ritual won't last forever. One day you'll find you have let go, you have trusted, that you feel more secure about your future and you won't have the anxiety or fear anymore. But if you ever need to return to the ritual, it will be there in your toolbox.

Journal

Do you have any rituals you use for coping? Create several and write in your journal how helpful they are.

Flowers by Day, Stars by Night: Finding Happiness after Loss and Change

Chapter 25
Exploring the Future

It's a challenge to think of a future without that person we've been with or without a certain situation we never thought would change. Because we believed, we didn't think it was possible that such darkness could set on our lives.

For instance, lives had been intricately combined, as they should have been because that's what marriage is about. It's the merging of two people into one relationship. But that also means that we never saw the day that it might end. Sometimes we also have become consumed in our lives with that person so much so that we don't have a life outside them. We have been involved with raising our families and might not have been working for a number of years. Our social lives revolved around them and we have neglected our friends. This makes us feel desperate and like a failure.

What we don't see, because the forest is too thick in front of us, is that there is a brilliant future, one filled with beautiful mountains or the ocean (whichever we prefer) waiting for us to enjoy. Others can see it but we don't because our pain is too deep.

It's at that time that we must start to explore the future. The longer we put it off the longer it will take for us to enjoy what should be ours.

Chapter 26
The Grateful Factor

We also have a tendency to focus on everything we don't have for ourselves. We are negative and look at what everyone else has, but we think we don't have any of it. And when we are faced with the loss of something, we watch people– especially families– go by us in a shopping mall or restaurant– and we believe they have it all because we have lost something. We are convinced of this even though we know nothing about them.

Somewhere along the line we were taught that no matter what we accomplished, there was always someone who had more than us. And in that process we stopped being grateful for what we have because we thought someone else always had more. While to some extent, this mentality can be helpful to drive us, when it becomes we are so focused on what we don't have, then it becomes a detriment.

No more. You aren't allowed to think those thoughts again– just the like negative thoughts about yourself. Instead, you need to focus on what you do have because the more realize you have in your life, the more you'll feel hopeful and happy.

While it's preferable to start your day this way, I understand that for some people it might be easier to do this in the evening.

Pull out your journal and title a page "All that I am thankful for." Then start listing everything you have in your life. Of course this can be your grandmother's china, but it's not just about material items. What about the people in your life? Who are you thankful for? And what have you accomplished? Look around you. Is the sun shining? Aren't you grateful for that?

What about the fact that last summer you dreamed of going off the high dive and finally did it? Ah, who cares that you were in your thirties that you did it. The important part is that you did and you're thankful you did because it makes you happy to think about. And it's been a good story to tell at gatherings with your friends.

I'm sure you're thankful for the fact that you can breathe, that you can walk, that you have food on the table.

Yes we have lost something in our lives, something we thought would be their forever, but we also have much to be thankful for. Each day look at this list and keep adding to it as you think of other items and aspects you're thankful for.

The more time you spend on this, the more you will see that you really do have a lot to be grateful for.

Journal

What are you grateful for?

Chapter 27
Identifying When You Feel Bad

It took me a long time to figure out what made me cranky and feel bad. I'm not talking about when something goes wrong with a bill or an appliance that isn't working. Those are inconveniences that are annoying. I'm referring to the times when we feel like picking a fight with someone or we think the world is against us. We feel insecure during those times.

For me they come when I'm tired and during the night. I only recently figured this out so be aware this might not happen overnight. One day I was not very happy, feeling frustrated with a variety of things, and I realized this isn't how I feel most of the time. I'm usually a pretty upbeat person. While I won't say that I jump out of bed in the morning, once I get out to run I feel pretty good. I admit that I enjoy the sounds of the birds singing and I have talked a lot about enjoying the light of a new day.

But sometimes people and events drain me in my life or I've been working hard and need a break. And there are the times I wake up in the middle of the night and can't go back to sleep so I start to think (which is more likely the reason I can't go back to sleep). I'm not a big fan of nighttime. Once I hit about dinner time I'm usually not good for much and it's better I go to bed and start over the next day. So if I'm awake during the night I think irrational things that would make no sense to my "regular" self.

Once I figured this out– realizing how much being rested and daylight were important to me– I am trying to remind myself when I feel that way how I need to be gentle with myself and focus on other things. Maybe I need to get some extra sleep that night or I need to read for a while. A lot of times going for a walk works really well for me. It's even better if I can leave the phone behind and not be disturbed by technology for an hour while my dog Hattie and I are out. Or swim. Something that reminds me of my hope.

It's important to know what your triggers are because you want to know what to do when those feelings surface.

Journal

What are the triggers that make you feel sad or depressed? How can you become aware of them? What can you do about them?

Flowers by Day, Stars by Night: Finding Happiness after Loss and Change

Chapter 28
Spinning Perspective

It's easy anywhere in our lives to focus on what we don't have. It's not just about being grateful for all aspects in our lives– as I discussed in the previous section– but that there is something to learn from any situation we find ourselves placed in. When a relationship ends, we lose someone we love, a job we love ends; it might feel like the end of the world. But it's not. It's all in how we look at it.

No matter what happens to us, life is still good and it means there is a new door to open. If at twenty-one, when my sister ended her life, I thought that there was nothing good left in life, I would have been in for a long terrible, sad, depressing road of life.

But while I was sad and angry that my sister died– and at times I felt as if my hope for my future had been taken from me– something inside me still burned. It was that ember of hope, a very small one, but it was still there nonetheless. And even as I grieved her death, I took my life forward. I went to classes (although not doing as well as I had before her death) and a few weeks later the summer internship I wanted so badly at the United States Olympic Training Center in Colorado Springs came to fruition. It was a challenging summer because I was grieving her death, but I made the most of it.

Some years ago I ran into a fellow intern in San Francisco and he was talking about what a great time he had that summer. He stopped and said, "But I know it wasn't a happy summer for you."

I stopped him and told him that mostly what I remember was the good. Yes, I can go through a list of challenges from that summer, but mostly I recall the good times and laughter. And the experiences I knew I'd never have again.

In the years of losses since then, it wasn't easy but I've always tried to remember there is good in no matter what happens. For the deaths in my life, it meant peace for my loved ones who didn't always feel peace here from the emotional or physical pain they endured. For the end of my marriage it meant lessons I could take forward to be a better partner and the opportunity for a new beginning with someone else in my life.

And I have learned that in the biggest challenges, to ask myself (or God during prayer) what I'm supposed to learn so that I can move forward from it and let it go. Often, situations keep happening to us because we're not learning from them. This is particularly true with relationships when we continually select partners who keep hurting us– or when we would like a partner but it doesn't seem to be happening.

Flowers by Day, Stars by Night: Finding Happiness after Loss and Change

By spinning it around (which can be painful because it forces us to see something good when we have been programmed only to see the bad in circumstances), by asking what good can come from it, by questioning what we can learn from it, by being grateful for what we do have, we will begin to realize there is still lots of good life ahead of us. Even though we never forget where we have been, the sun still shines on us and warms our skin.

Journal

Where in your life can you spin a situation around and see the good that has come out of it? Where can you do this now? If you don't see anything positive now, leave room to write something and keep coming back until you find something positive. It's there but you might not see it yet.

Chapter 29
Finding Inspiration

It began with motivational sayings, usually ones that I drew from my favorite pop songs. When I took up running at age twelve, joining my junior high cross country team that fall, I quickly learned I had to figure out a way to fill what I call the "mental space" during a run that lasted anywhere from two to six miles. One of my favorite songs was John Parr's "St. Elmo's Fire" from the movie of the same name. If I couldn't play the song in my Sony Walkman, then I had to sing it in my head. It's called "checking out," a way to keep myself motivated to keep running, even when it hurt or I just didn't feel like doing it.

As I moved into high school and running took up a bigger presence in my life, I started to make what people now call "dream boards." For me I was looking for a way to inspire myself with something to look at. I cut out words and pictures from magazines (and sometimes newspapers) and glued them onto large pieces of paper and made collages that I hung in my room. I still have these today. Although they are packed in a closet, if I pull them out, I know I would find most of the sayings and pictures still inspiring.

I didn't know it at the time, but the ways that I inspired myself then are ways I still use today. On a wall in my office, I have several pages I have torn from magazines that I find inspiring: these are usually swimming pools scenes. Or they might be of dresses that I wish I had (or had a reason to wear).

I try to surround myself with what inspires me: the shelves in my office are lined with items that constitute not just my life but me. These include the ceramic M that my mom painted yellow and then added pink dots ("M is for mumps" she said– and then I contracted them). I have a box of Crayola 64 crayons that I hardly ever use but reminds me of the importance of drawing in my life. There are books, mugs filled with various pens, a collection of several ceramic dogs I have gathered over the years, and several photos. These items might not mean anything to anyone else but they do to me and when I stand in there and look around, it inspires me to keep doing what's important to me: writing and creating. It's also what keeps me going on days when I feel sad or overwhelmed by life events.

When we are experiencing a loss, it's easy to forget what inspires us because all we can think about is our loss. This is one important place that is also about spinning perspective: it's a challenge but somehow we need to refocus from what we have lost to what we still have.

Journal

What inspires you?

Flowers by Day, Stars by Night: Finding Happiness after Loss and Change

Chapter 30
Finding Peace

We don't feel at peace when we have experienced a loss. In fact, we don't like how we feel. We want our old, comfortable life back. We want our routine as we knew it back. We want to know that person is there for us. We want, we want.

The reality is that we can't have it back. We can pine for it all we want but that won't change it. While the memories are ours, the future ahead of us is not the one that we imagined. That often is enough to make people feel as if there is no reason to go on.

But there is! The key is that we have to find peace in our lives again. Not just an overall sense of peace, but peace in the empty spaces. These spaces include when we are alone on a Friday night, when we wake up in the morning and it takes a moment to remember how life has changed. Or on Saturday morning when we realize we don't have plans for the day.

Before our life changed, we had activities, we had someone we spent time with, and now we are alone.

But no one can change that for us: we have to find ways to fill those empty spaces. Are there any activities or hobbies you've stopped doing that you once enjoyed? Even if you can't read a book because your mind is stumbling all over the place, maybe there is something you can focus on. A magazine might provide for a quicker read (even celebrity gossip can be a short distraction and enough to be reminded how good your life is). Do you like to give yourself manicures or pedicures? Have you put that off for some time? These aren't supposed to be sweeping changes in the small spaces of your life. The key is to make steps so that one day they look like big movements but really you've been moving forward all along. Kind of like the overnight sensation who has been working at it for ten years. When we get to goal setting, we'll also talk more about this.

Figure out what times of day are most challenging for you. If it's in the evening after work and after dinner (and you need something to keep you from reaching for the potato chips or the bottle of wine after you've done the dishes, left the kitchen, and turned on the television), then figure out a way to distract yourself. If you can exercise in the evening, maybe go for a walk (and take your dog or kids with you). Read something. Work on a craft project.

If you have trouble sleeping or when you wake up in the morning, you might try meditating or prayer. This could be a time to write in your journal. Reflect on the day: what was hard and what did you learn from it? What was good and how can you make sure more good happens to you?

If Friday evening or Saturday morning are challenging, what kinds of activities can you plan? Who do you have in your life that is a positive influence you can spend time with? You want to be with people who are positive and help you grow, not hold you back. Go to the movies, download a movie, get lost in a story for a while. Go for a long walk on Saturday morning or go to a museum or some sort of historic site. There are lots of activities to do on weekends that are free or cost very little. You have to keep all parts of yourself active: emotionally, physically, spiritually, and intellectually. There is plenty of time for rest, but if you are feeling less than peaceful, then those are the times to find peace through something that makes you feel good.

Journal

What times of day are the most challenging for you? What can you do to change them?

Activity

Challenge yourself to make one change this upcoming week. Keep track of how well you do: each day mark whether or not you did it and how it made you feel when you completed it. Do you feel more peaceful the more you do the activity? Continue to make smaller changes in your life and document them. If something doesn't work, then try something else.

Chapter 31
Choosing Supportive People

For some people, this will be one of the biggest challenges in this book. We have surrounded ourselves with people who might not be the best support. This could be because these are people who have been our friends for a long time and we are comfortable with them. However, it could be that we wallow in each other's pain rather than help each other grow. Or it could be that we are biologically related and find that we can't force people out of our lives because they are family.

If your biological family doesn't treat you well and you don't feel like you can cut them out of your life, then at least learn to draw a line in the sand. Often the people who treat us the worst are our families because they take advantage of us. They aren't happy people and take it out on someone they know won't go away. But if we want to go forward in life, we have to learn to keep them emotionally at a distance because they will not be happy about us making ourselves better. Instead, they will try to sabotage it by continually putting us down. Jealous friends might do the same because they don't want to move forward so they don't want you to as well.

An ex-husband might try to break you down even though you are divorced. If you don't have children and have untangled your lives, then don't have contact with him if he isn't supportive. Same for an ex-boyfriend. If you have children together and he is a part of their lives, then look for ways to keep him at a distance. The stronger you are, in time he will learn that he can't hurt you. He'll see that you're not the person he walked all over before. Eventually he'll give up and move onto someone else. It doesn't matter who, that's not your problem because you can't change him. All that matters is that you take care of yourself because you're looking forward and not back.

Who are the supportive people in your life? Who is cheering you on as you make these positive changes? Who is truly there for you? Usually it's not the people you think it will be. In times of loss, people don't know what to say, sometimes they are too scared to say something at all and drift away, or the loss might remind them that they could be you and that will cause them to appear distant. Or because your relationship status might have changed, maybe they aren't including you in previous couple activities anymore. When there is a divorce, people tend to "pick a side." They will say this won't happen but it does.

It hurts but remember that each time a door closes, a new one opens. And as you close many of them, that means there are many doors to open. You have friends who have maybe felt more like acquaintances, but if they are people who are standing next to you, being supportive friends, then let them. Maybe they've been in a similar situation as you and know what it's like to feel like you do. While no one can walk in another person's shoes, what we can do is walk in similar shoes.

And if you don't feel like you have any friends at all, then find ways to make new friends. There are other people out there like you– after all, you're not the only person reading this book– looking for the same friendships. As you add new activities to your life, you'll find friends there. Or maybe you have some neighbors who would like to get together for a walk once a week.

You aren't as alone as you think you are.

Journal

Where do you need to make changes with the supports in your life?

Activity

Reach out to one new or old friend a week and suggest you go out for coffee or for a walk. They might not all stick, but the more effort you put into it, the more positive outcome you'll see.

Chapter 32
The Forgiveness Journey

We have been taught that we should forgive. And we've been taught that this should be something easy to do, like we can easily forgive someone who has hurt us and that once we give them our forgiveness we will move on.

Well, if it were that easy, most people would not be walking around with pain and anger inside of them. People might say, "But I did forgive him for how he hurt me. I told him. And I moved on."

Yet it's obvious that even entering into a new relationship, this person is still angry over what happened and sometimes it bubbles up when they least expect it. And then they wonder, "But I forgave him? Why do I still hurt?" Or they might deny they hurt and still feel hurt, believing that having said they forgave the person— as they were taught to do.

Other people wonder how years can go by and they still feel hurt, believing that time heals all wounds. It doesn't unless you put the effort into healing those wounds.

That doesn't mean that forgiveness is easy though! It means letting go of something we've been holding in our tightly clenched fist as if it's a million dollars. This isn't a million dollars we want to keep though. These million dollars are filled with bad energy, pain, and ill feelings.

There are aspects that forgiveness is not: when we forgive, it doesn't mean we say that it was okay to not treat us well. It doesn't mean that we condone that behavior. It also doesn't mean that we have to communicate with the other person when we forgive them for their actions.

Instead, this is something we do for *us*. We don't need to have a conversation with that person about it nor do we say it was okay to treat us badly.

What forgiveness is: the ability to say that we want to move on and we don't harbor those ill feelings of what happened.

That sounds easy enough, right? But now we have to get there. This is the part that will take some work.

Remember, this is about you and not that other person. This is about soothing the hurt inside you, not because it was okay to be treated badly, but because it's keeping you from moving forward.

First you need to acknowledge what causes the hurt and pain. What did this person do? You also should look back in your past and see if anyone else had done something similar earlier that you might need to forgive as well because the two are now intertwined. Take the time to tease them apart. Perhaps you were making the second person suffer because of something that someone else did to you before and your perception of the event was different than what really happened. Or maybe both really hurt you and you never realized that they had become one big clump of anger through time.

If there are any previous situations involved you will need to work at forgiving the first situation to start. There are a variety of ways to do this but, always remember this is about you. This does not mean you will talk to that person because the reality is that the other person involved probably either doesn't care or is in another place with his life.

Think about the ways that this person hurt you: Was it emotional? Physical? What is it about the way that you were treated that still hurts you so much? These probing questions are not meant to be easy because you must process through them to admit to yourself what really happened. And you have to let go of any comfort that this pain gives you. You might think that hurting that person emotionally in some way will make you feel better, but my guess is that if you had the chance to do it, it wouldn't help. You'd still be feeling bad.

Whatever you want from that person you will not get and that's why this must be about you. Don't think that if they say they are sorry you will be able to move on. Someone can tell you he is sorry all day long, but you could still harbor resentment. Spin it around: What will help you let go of the resentment?

Not forgiving someone isn't productive. Look at any person you know who has someone they haven't forgiven. If you spend a little time talking with them or observing them, you'll realize that not forgiving that person is like the final puzzle piece to them having a truly healthy, happy life. Harboring that kind of pain isn't productive and also can cause physical and emotional health issues.

The reasons are endless to be angry with someone who hurt us. It's challenging to understand why someone who showed us love and affection, who promised to be there for us, one day decided not to be with us. We don't get how someone fell out of love with us or where that person we cared so much for went. How could things be so different? Or why someone left our lives.

That's why we are angry, hurt, sad, and a million other emotions we have already discussed. No more though. I have given you time to acknowledge the emotions. Now it's time to let it go. My hope is that by the time you have gotten to this point in the book, you have been able to let go of your fear of the unknown or at least you have been able to acknowledge that fear.

Now though, it's time to stop thinking about the person or situation that hurt you. No more calling them names. No more telling the stories about the awful stuff they did to you.

No more being angry at how you felt you were treated.

The people you know (and you could be one of them) who have never been able to forgive their former partner are the people in your life who are stuck. They go into new relationships but the new partner is turned off by the angry words about the former partner. No one wants to be with someone who is that negative. And if they talk about the person that way, what will they say about us behind our backs?

If the person continues to be antagonistic in our lives, don't engage them. Remember, they know how to push our buttons best because of our relationship with them. They know how we are manipulated. By not engaging them, refusing to play their game, we are getting back the upper hand. It's not as much fun when we don't want to play with them. They will quickly lose interest and leave us alone.

This is a test, as in not answering text messages/phone calls, saying no when they ask for money or a favor, or just generally trying to figure out what's going on in their lives. Gossiping about them is not relative to our lives. Sure, we think we'll feel good to know they are struggling but ultimately it doesn't help us any.

Whatever it takes, like pinching ourselves or putting a dollar in a jar each time we think about them (and donate the funds to a charity) or want to respond to a text or phone call, find some way to distract yourself from them. When we feel angry, do some physical exercise that makes us too tired to care about how we felt before we started.

This process will help you to forgive. The less you think about that person, what they are up to, and how they hurt you, the more you will find yourself not caring about them. We shouldn't have time to worry about their lives anyway. Our time should be spent thinking about how are making our lives even better than they are. What is it we are doing for ourselves and for others? If we still can't answer those questions, then we need to devote more time to those tasks and take up the effort we keep putting into wondering whom the former partner is dating or how they are spending their money.

If someone has died, we need to forgive him or her for leaving us. It's the past and it needs to be left there. You can still have greatness ahead of you– if you choose it.

There are other ways to cope with lingering feelings toward that person. Write them a letter and tell them why we feel hurt. The key is not to send it! Burn it, a ritual in itself, as a way of letting them go. Write down as many times possible that we forgive them. "I forgive _____." It's like the sentences we got in school– writing them over and over helped us not to do again what we did before, right? Do it at least twenty-five times. And then do it again the next day. And the next day. Or write it one hundred times in one day. Light a candle and ask for help forgiving them.

Think of ways that have helped you cope in the past let go of something or someone, and draw on past experience of what worked or alter what you did before so that it works this time.

It's not worth it to drink heavily or abuse alcohol or drugs. People who do it wake up the next day feeling just as bad if not worse. It numbs the pain but only for a short period of time. Without coping with it, it will come back.

When we forgive, we will find that closing the door, to say we wish them well, then we have finally put that final piece in the puzzle to sealing the door shut.

However, we aren't finished by forgiving them. We also need to forgive ourselves. Sometimes this is more of a challenge, especially for those of us who are hard on ourselves. We beat ourselves up for every little decision we have made, sometimes even the good ones because we always believe we could have done better.

Are you angry with yourself for allowing him to treat you that way? Are you angry because of what you lost (emotional, material, etc.) after the relationship ended? Are you angry because you missed something he was doing and if you had caught it you would have ended the relationship long before? Are you angry with yourself, feeling stupid that you knew better but let it go on? There are a variety of different reasons you feel the way you do. Take the time to really think about them. There is probably more than what is on the surface, what you've allowed others to see. And if I had to guess, you're mostly mad at yourself for staying in a relationship that had something that wasn't working and you can't believe you didn't catch it.

Some days, especially when the storm is the darkest, it feels as if every decision we made was a bad one. There was always something better we could have done.

None of it is true. We made the best decision we could in the moment we were in or in that particular time of our life. We did the best we could with the skills we had at the time. Continuing to chastise ourselves even years after a decision, like marrying the person we did, is useless to our lives. It doesn't help us live a full life; rather it keeps us stuck in the past.

As children we beat ourselves up over things because this was sometimes how we learned. But many of us keep doing it because we feel like we need to be perfect. Remember, we all look back and can see what we did that didn't work out well. That's easy and any person can do that. The people who make the most of their lives see the lessons they learned, how the decisions they made (good or bad) made them who they are today. And they take that to propel life forward. That's who you should be.

Forgiveness means you draw boundaries. It means you don't let that hurt get to you again. It means you detach emotions from what happened. In the relationship there were good times and those are yours to keep. No one can take away anything you want to keep that is good. But you do not have to hold onto the outcome, especially if someone made a choice to end it with you.

You probably also feel hurt because you feel betrayed. You thought you would have a long life with this person. They were supposed to grow old with you. While cheating on someone is a big betrayal, sometimes the bigger betrayal is the loss of the future. In that loss of the future, you might have lost money, a home, hope, happiness, and possibly some of your friends.

This is the time to let all that go. If you still feel challenged by this, return to the chapter about gratefulness. I doubt anyone can do any of the work in this book once and truly move forward. It's like learning to ride a bicycle: you're going to fall off a few times before it takes hold. But once it does, you'll be riding off into the sunset with your freedom.

Tell yourself, mumbling over and over again, that you forgive yourself, that you had no idea you were still hurting this much.

And then stop. You've had enough time to think about it. Now we need to go forward.

Forgive yourself for decisions you made, words you spoke, or actions you made. They aren't worth thinking about. They are done and there is too much life to live to think back about what you did. Think instead about what you can *do*.

Journal

Who do you need to forgive? How will you do this?

Flowers by Day, Stars by Night: Finding Happiness after Loss and Change

Chapter 33
Anger

There is a menu of emotions you are experiencing; there might be one that you feel more often than another and for most people that's anger.

The anger wells up when we least expect it or sometimes we find ourselves feeling angry all the time. Anger is the overriding emotion because it protects us from further pain. We are angry with the other person, the world, and the situation, even the checker at the store because she can't ring up our groceries right. We believe most of our anger is directed at the other person for changing our lives. Even if the person died, we're mad he left us because this was not the life that we were supposed to have.

Mostly though– and what we are afraid to admit– is we are angry with ourselves.

We're angry with ourselves for allowing a wide range of things to happen. We wonder how we let the relationship get to that point because clearly in our minds anything that happened was our fault. We might have been told it was our fault or our past history in our families of being blamed for events that happened (even when they had nothing to do with us, we were just an easy target). We also don't think we should enjoy anything good because we don't think it ever comes our way.

So we shut down. And we become angry.

We do this to protect ourselves because it feels that the only way to escape painful feelings is to become angry. We are feeling something when we're angry and that's better than not feeling anything at all.

However, we end up staying angry and we find we can't let it go to move forward. Some people will say anger is motivating but it is only to a point. It might be what initially gets us moving, but at some point we get so angry we can't do anything else but be angry. That's when we flop ourselves onto the couch and give up.

We think we're better off there, again, because we're protecting ourselves. Really all we're doing is delaying moving forward and using anger as an excuse.

The key is figuring out what the anger we feel stems from. Is it really what the person in the relationship did or is it something much deeper that happened a long time ago? Are we punishing someone for something he did when it wasn't all about him, there was also something else in the past that started it? We need to stop being accusatory with people and explore why we are angry. We need to untangle our anger into forgiveness.

Journal

Spend time writing in your journal about anger, Make a list of events/situations that make you feel angry. This might take a week or two as you think about them, but as you look over the list, I'm guessing you will start to see a pattern. And begin to understand where the root of that anger was planted.

And when you feel angry as you do this, it's important to take a breath, a step back, and start to realize that you need to change it. Use this as a direct exercise for the next section about managing your emotions.

Go for a walk or talk to someone. No more will you let the anger boil inside of you. It's time to throw that pot of water off the stove and move onto other things that are more productive and will make you happy.

Chapter 34
Managing Emotions and Coping

It's important that we know how to cope with the pain and hurt we feel. If we don't manage our emotions, they will overwhelm us and shut us down.

This will take time so don't expect immediate change. However, by making little changes, you will slowly notice over time that you're doing better. We've already talked about coping as we have gone along and hopefully you've already begun to integrate changes into your life. Don't beat yourself up if you miss something or forget. It's no different than learning something new: you're going to fall down or off the bicycle. Changing behavior isn't easy and that's exactly what you're learning to do here with the exercises in this guide.

The first step is to be aware of the negative emotions that we feel. By being aware of them, something that will take time, we then can identify that we need to make change.

So what do you do when you feel angry, sad, hurt?

That's when most people shut down. For me, it depends on the type of hurt I have experienced. I'll be honest and say that usually when I'm hurt, I will be angry for a while and sometimes the emotions may pass periodically for weeks, even months, sometimes years. However, mostly I will allow myself time to feel sorry for myself and then I will get over it and think about what I can do to make change in my life.

Why? Because I learned a long time ago that when someone hurts us, it's not worth dwelling about. The best thing we can do is make ourselves better. While I don't wish anything bad on anyone, I know that I can take my life further and higher rather than wallowing in what I have lost. This lesson was taught to me in sixth grade when my neighborhood elementary school friends decided to unfriend me (obviously not a term we were using the early eighties). I can say I am not angry with them now and I do talk to some of them, but they did some things that weren't very nice.

They simply decided I wasn't good enough to be their friend. They shunned me from anything they did together, but because some of us were Catholic we were still in the same religion class carpool, which was very lonely for me since they didn't talk to me. They created a secret admirer and put notes in the mailbox and said it was from him (as if I couldn't figure out the handwriting) and would ask me about it.

More than anything it was a very lonely time. The first thing I did was reach out to a girl who I knew lived close to me and ask her if she wanted to do things. Although she moved away about a year later that was the start of finding new friends.

But the big change was that summer after sixth grade when I decided to run track.

I was never very good at anything athletic. I had long legs and often stood like a flamingo but I also was short and not very coordinated (wearing glasses didn't help). Everything I did in track I pretty much finished last. But I was lucky that I had a coach who was good about encouraging me and because of him I kept at it.

That fall I went out for the cross country team– having no clue what it meant– and although I was one of the slowest runners at the start of the season, by the end of it I was part of a team that helped win the city championship. When I went out for the cross country team in high school, again I was the slowest runner on the team, but by the end of the season I surprised even my coach and ended up on varsity, earning a varsity letter in the process.

I had new friends by now. I had also earned the respect of the girls who had been so unfriendly to me several years before. While our friendships were never the same again, we could be casually nice to each other and I was okay with that.

The experience taught me the importance of not giving up when life or people hurt me. I realize that it might take time but something new will come along when I let something (or someone) go. Sometimes the doors that open are the ones we least expect, but if we allow ourselves to be open to new experiences we can develop life long friends, experiences, hobbies, whatever it may be.

When I lived back in my hometown for about a year and a half after my divorce, I went to Mass almost every day of the week (I joked that I gave myself Saturdays off). I did this because I was having such a hard time living with my mom who never went anywhere and I was dealing with some challenging situations regarding men in my life. Some of them were much too complicated, but I wasn't willing at the time to give up on them. My fear of the unknown had me clinging to relationships I should have long broken.

I always thought that people who went to daily Mass were a little weird (which included my grandmother), but I also knew that at least it was something positive I could do. And so I would sit there and be sad, angry, and hurt. Mass was at 8:00 am and the goal was that I allowed myself to feel that way during Mass, then I could go home and get to work and not think about it the rest of the day. While it didn't work all the time, at least it was a step in the right direction of giving myself time to feel bad, to wallow in it, and try to give it to God (that part was much easier said than done). It became one coping mechanism for me.

Another one I mentioned before: going for a walk. Sometimes it's good to get out and I would do that even if it was thirty degrees and the wind was blowing. I can't say that I enjoyed it but at least it got me outside and gave me time to let my thoughts wander. And usually by the time I got home after walking my dogs for almost three miles, I felt better. I came up with ideas during those walks for my writing or other things I wanted to accomplish. Mostly I gave myself the freedom to let my mind wander which is probably what I needed most.

Journal

What can you use to distract yourself, to bring you out of your hurt?

Identify and write down when you feel hurt/angry/sad. Write down any triggers you believe bring it on. Then write down a list of ways you can help yourself cope with these emotions. Work on these coping methods and revisit your journal to make notations about whether or not they worked. Remember, the first one might not work and you might need to try several ways before something sticks for you.

Flowers by Day, Stars by Night: Finding Happiness after Loss and Change

Chapter 35
Other Emotions and Seeking Help

There are a range of other emotions you might feel when you're alone, like sadness and depression. These are very typical and very much expected; After all, this is reason to be sad and depressed. That is part of the grieving process because that's exactly what this is: a process of letting go, but we can't do that without feeling the bumps under us. Some of these bumps are the ones that leave us crying all the time.

However, if the depression– the lack of hope– goes on for a long period of time, that might be the time to seek bigger help. If you find that you can't get out of bed for a series of days or feel so hopeless that you have thoughts of hurting yourself, then you need to find help.

There are a lot of great therapists out there, as there are great medications that can help you through a hard time. I've known people to take anti-depressants for just a short time, enough to get them through this part of the grieving process. Then they go off them and go on with their lives.

When looking for a therapist, ask for referrals, but know that it's okay to therapist shop. You might not like the first one you meet or you might find after two sessions that it's not going to work. Give it a chance but if you really don't feel comfortable, ask yourself why. You might be uncomfortable because the therapist is forcing you to face emotions and feelings you would rather sweep under a bed. Then you should stay. But there also are therapists who aren't as good and you have a sense that it's not helping. You want someone who gives you homework, who questions you, who wants to see you go forward, not someone who simply listens and keeps you coming back to the same story each week without any movement forward.

However, don't give up on therapy. Many people do because they think it didn't work out with the first therapist so it won't work out with any therapist. Finding a therapist isn't much different than finding a life partner. Not everyone marries the first person they meet.

Chapter 36
Fear

It's easy to use any emotion to cover up for fear. Anyone can do this easily.

But why do we fear everything? Haven't we finally learned that life does work out? That no matter how much we fear something, we end up holding ourselves back or we realize that we wasted a whole lot of energy on something when we could have been more productive.

I've had a lot of situations happen to me where I instantly got upset, fearful, and worried. I thought they were the end of the world, that life would never be the same again.

Then after they were over, I realized that I had wasted too much energy on something that was pointless. This then annoyed me because I already know how short life is and I know better than to get so afraid.

While I'm not perfect, I believe I have gotten much better about not reacting to things or letting them overwhelm me. I try to keep it in perspective and as you will read about shortly, having a higher power to "give" my fears to has helped. I now realize that there are things I can do and things I can't do and I try to focus on what I can do.

I also remember the prayer by St. Theresa that reminds me that there is no reason to live in fear, that all is well. I use "all as well" as a mantra when I am afraid of something. But it's been a journey to remind myself of this and not get overwhelmed by whatever is happening.

We are afraid of many things in life and after any kind of loss, especially that of a relationship, one of the biggest ones is being alone. There is truth to balancing believing in a future together with someone while also knowing that we should appreciate each day we have with anyone who is in our lives.

If we take life with someone for granted, and then it ends, that's where the fear kicks in. Fear makes us insecure because that's what fear wants. It encourages us to be afraid of the future, of being alone, or having a miserable rest of our lives.

And that's exactly why we should let fear go and face it straight on.

We need to make fear powerless in our lives. You've already started the road to this by reading this book and doing earlier exercises. Fear is not something to be, well, feared. The more you complete the exercises and lessons in this book, the more you'll find yourself not just staring down fear, but walking right past it with a smirk.

This isn't to say that you won't ever be afraid again. You will– that's reality. But what will

Flowers by Day, Stars by Night: Finding Happiness after Loss and Change

happen is that you'll find fewer experiences will leave you afraid. When those that do come along, you'll have better tools to handle them.

A small amount of fear is good, too. After all, we need to find ourselves motivated to do something. We might be afraid when we walk to the starting line of our first 10K run or walk, thinking, what have I done? Am I really going to traverse six miles? But its that little bit of fear that will boost you up and give you the adrenalin to complete the course.

And when you're done, you'll wonder, I was afraid of *that*?

Journal

What are you afraid of? How are you working to overcome it?

Chapter 37
Balance

We aren't just emotional beings. The common thought is that if we take care of our emotional selves, we're taking care of all of us. And there was a time I believed this. However, the reality is that we are holistic people. We need to balance our emotional, physical, spiritual, and intellectual selves.

I know that on the outside I have always looked like a person who had life in balance. But in the past four years I learned how much I was neglecting my spiritual self. Sure, I run each day, I say a prayer for gratefulness and mention what wants and needs I have. I write in a journal and talk to various people to keep my emotional self in check. And intellectually I am always reading up and learning about something new.

But I found out that even though I was doing a short prayer each morning, it wasn't enough. Of course I thought it was but as I returned back to mass on a weekly basis (even going daily for a period of time), I then saw how much peace it brought me. And when I added a five-minute prayer (Gasp! How could anyone pray for five minutes I always wondered) with a candle most mornings, I saw the difference it made in how I coped with the day ahead of me.

However, it also looked as if I was taking good care of myself physically and emotionally on the outside. But after several years of lingering stress over the losses in my life, and my continued energy into trying to keep everything status quo, I developed fibroids in my uterus. This caused non-stop bleeding that began to filter into my emotional health. While I continued to live my life, most people didn't know the challenge I was faced with (and I'm learning that many women cope with as well).

During surgery to burn my uterus lining out, it was discovered that I had a golf-ball sized fibroid in my uterus. This one had eluded the ultrasound and surprised the doctor who had gone in prepared for something else. Instead of burning out the uterus lining, he spent my time in surgery removing that large fibroid.

When I came out of surgery and in the weeks ahead, I began acupuncture to work to keep my body in balance. While I had been doing it for a about a year and a half before the surgery, I had a new doctor, one who had been a gynecologist in China before coming to the United States.

"You have too much stress," she said, adding, "You're too young to be this stressed."

You don't know my life, I wanted to say. But I knew this meant something larger. I didn't want to be back where I was with the bleeding. That meant I had to make some changes in my life. Everything about us works in balance; all pieces of us are tied together. And if I want to have that balance– so that it doesn't send any part of me out of whack– I'm going to have to do a better job managing my stress. That means making time for each piece of me. And while it will never equally add up to 100% each day, I need to be aware that if I'm spending most of my day at my desk, maybe I need a little more physical activity.

While I haven't made a lot of large changes, I've started running harder again and swimming in the afternoon. I have my five-minute prayer in the morning. And I'm always working at finding more time to read. I believe it sometimes is about the small changes that make the biggest difference in the long run.

I'm also making sure that I give myself time for my creative outlets each day. While I write most days, I found I needed to get back to other kinds of art and took up painting in the last year. Recently I've returned to sewing. Much of my day is scheduled out because it's the only way I can fit everything in. What works for me might not work for every other person, but through trial and error– and experience– I have gotten a good idea of what I need to do. Now it's just keeping with it, which is always easier said that done. And it means sometimes we have to give something up.

Journal

Where do you need to work on balance in your life?

Chapter 38
Your Physical Self

I know a few people are cringing when they are starting to read this section. That probably means this section is for you.

When we have loss in our lives, one of the first aspects to go is any physical exercise. We feel tired, we feel confused. We are angry, sad, depressed. And we forget that our bodies need the physical self to get a workout to feel better. Getting out of bed is hard enough, but the idea of going to the gym, much less a walk out the front door, feels impossible. And we find we don't care. If our loved ones left us then what reason do we have to care about how we look?

If you're already exercising, then look at whether what you're doing is enough. Maybe you need to tweak it or take on a new activity. Or maybe you need to work more on what you're eating. It's good occasionally to take a step back and reevaluate especially if you have reached a plateau and you haven't quite hit your goals.

Even if you are taking a walk each day that's a good start. Being out with nature is good; getting your body to move is even better. And in bad weather there is always the treadmill (although I am a fan of getting outside no matter what the weather is unless it's dangerous). But don't be content just to walk. Think about how you can walk faster. What kind of goals can you set? Maybe sign up for a 5K walk that you can work up to. Or a 10K if you can easily walk a 5K. Or start to jog a few steps each day.

There are other means of exercise: join a gym and find a trainer if you aren't sure what to do. Ask a friend to meet you at the gym if you're someone who won't exercise if you don't have a commitment with someone else. Start swimming. You probably have a bicycle in the garage you haven't used in a long time. There are lots of ways to get exercise. Find one that works for you.

This also would be a time where you could learn to do something new. I took up golf, surfing, and returned to tennis. I had taken tennis lessons in junior high, but never really played after that. Once when a friend and I were out playing on a summer morning not long after I started playing again, a lady playing on the next court said she had given it up in her early twenties and had just picked it back up in her seventies.

It's never too late.

Exercise is a good time to think about your goals, about your future, talk to God, let your mind wander. It's also a good way to start your day– while exercise at first might make you feel more tired, eventually you'll find you have more energy. And you can spend time nurturing your spiritual and emotional sides as well.

Some people put weight on during times of loss for a variety of reasons but the biggest one is that they don't care. They will say they don't have the energy to take care of themselves and of course this is true, you don't have a lot of energy because it's being eaten up by your emotional side, which is trying to cope with the changes.

But this is not the time to abandon exercise because it's much harder to take off the weight than it was to put it on. The only way your energy is going to change is by doing something about it and the first step is to step out the front door and go for a walk. Rest in nature, even if there is snow on the ground. You've been feeling a lot of pain and now you can feel the elements around you. Enjoy them and relish in them.

You don't have to push your body hard at first; the initial step is doing something because that something is better than nothing.

You'll find after the walk that you feel better and sometimes having that time to let your mind wander helps. For me, checking out and thinking about what I'm going to write that day makes my run feel as if it takes less time. But when I walk or swim in the afternoons I let my mind wander as a way of rest after concentrating on work all day.

Exercise also is good because it forces you to connect with people. Yes, I know it's the last thing you want to do. But remember, just because you talk to someone on your walk doesn't mean you have to share your life story. You're probably just discussing the sunshine or your dog that's along for the trek.

And after you walk away from that person? You'll feel better. We feel deserted by our situation and we find we don't want to open up to anyone but humans aren't meant to be alone. There's a reason we marry and couple up: because we are meant to share our lives. So share your life— or at least say hi to the elderly guy trimming his hedges when you walk by on a sunny afternoon.

Exercise will bring you more energy but you must stick to it. You don't need to do it every day— find a routine that works for you. Consult a friend who has some knowledge about weight loss. Take a day off once a week, whatever is your busiest day. Or take Sunday off since it is traditionally thought of as a day of rest.

You already know what a difference sleep makes in your life. I'll be the first to admit that when I don't sleep, my view of the world is much darker and I don't function as well. It's understandable if you're having sleep issues. However, you need to do something about it because it's probably not going to go away for some time.

Whether you're having trouble falling asleep or you're waking up in the middle of the night and not able to go back to sleep, there is help. But also remember that as you process through this experience and your life morphs and changes— for the positive!— your sleep will come back.

In the meantime, you have options. For some people, they will get a prescription of a sleep medication. The key is not to be on it forever. You want something you can take temporarily so you can sleep and feel rested.

There are other options before you do that though. Start by looking at your sleep situation: Are you going to bed at a good hour? While some people can look at any sort of technology before they go to bed, for some of us it will keep us awake. I learned early on that I couldn't read a book on my ipad. If that's the case, then make sure that an hour before you want to sleep, you put away the phone, turn off the television, etc. And no eating in bed or eating late.

Take a book to bed— even if you fall asleep reading it that would be a good thing.

There are lots of other ways to help your sleep: make sure your room is cool, that your pets leave you plenty of room, and you're going to bed close to the same time each night. It's easy to get into a vicious cycle where you don't sleep, then you're tired all day, then you nap, then you can't sleep. There's also a lot of good information available on how to sleep better. If you do a Google search you will come up with articles.

And if you wake up in the middle of the night, you might try using this as a time of prayer. We will talk more about prayer in the spiritual piece but if you're laying in bed and you know you need to go to sleep but you keep looking at your clock and you see the minutes going by, that's not going to be helpful.

What is helpful is to use the time for something useful. Some people might get up and read (or for me, I have gotten up to write and usually the next night I am able to sleep) or another activity that will help you get tired. Hopefully after a night of being up, the next night you can sleep. However, I don't advocate for emptying the dishwasher like my mom used to do because there were other people in the house.

If you don't want to get out of bed though, then be careful not to let your mind wander into the negativity of your past. It's an easy time to feel like the world is against you, that you've been wronged, and that life isn't going to get better. This is just darkness trying to get to you. When the sun comes up, you know you always feel better and the feelings dissipate, but they don't when you're lying there alone in the dark watching your clock.

You can use this time to talk to God about how frustrated you are (even about how you don't understand why you can't sleep) or any other worries in your life. You also can tell him what you want, what you want to accomplish, who you want to be. And it's okay to tell him that you don't know how you will make it happen. After all, he's there to help you.

Whatever you do, make it a time where you're moving forward, not stuck on rehashing the pain of the past. And if you catch yourself doing that, make sure you stop and redirect yourself.

Sleeping better will help your perspective.

But when you're taking care of yourself physically, you also should be aware of what you're putting in your body. After a loss, who wants to cook when it feels like every ounce of energy is going into getting through the day? It's easier to stop for fast food or break open a bag of chips. And once that routine starts, it's hard to break out of it, especially because junk food is addicting in many ways: it leaves us wanting more.

If you have a hard time working toward eating better, find a friend who can help. There are phone apps where people can be accountable to each other both with eating and exercise. With eating, work with a friend to come up with doable snacks: the kind that taste good and are filling. It's great to eat lots of vegetables but we still need some fats (like nuts) and carbohydrates (whole grains) to help us feel full.

Most of eating well is rooted in planning. By taking a lunch to work (and snacks), you're less likely to hit the vending machine for the chips or the candy bars.

Make sure to eat breakfast. Everything you've heard about a good breakfast is true. And once your body adjusts to getting more food during the day, it will want less that night. However, eating at night also is a habit that needs to be broken. This goes back to finding activities to keep us busy instead of surveying what's in the cabinets and the freezer.

Is what you're eating giving you adequate nutrition to at least keep you full for several hours? Although not everyone is a morning person, life generally runs on morning being an important part of our day so we want to make sure we have the energy for the morning. While we have traditionally encouraged people to eat bagels and cereal for breakfast, the carbohydrates sometimes make people sleepier.

Instead, you want protein: eggs, nuts. You want a little fat: cheese, avocado, nuts. And you want low-sugar fruit: berries. My breakfast for a period of time was blueberries, a few slices of cheese, and walnuts.

Finally, I never tell anyone to completely get rid of junk food unless it's a life or death health reason. Depriving yourself of something you love will only haunt you later when you eat an entire bag of chips or eat a carton of ice cream. Instead, use it as a treat. I remember when McDonald's was a treat in my family: it was somewhere Mom took us about three times a year, not somewhere that people eat daily like they do today. Junk food should be treated the same way in our lives. It's your reward for working hard.

And when you do it, keep it in moderation. You'll enjoy it and look forward to the next time without feeling gluttonous. And if you don't have self control, then ask someone to keep the candy bars for you where you can't find them.

Because of the losses, our bodies are asking for more energy, but energy that is nutrient rich that will help sustain us. Not only are we grieving the loss, but we're also trying to function at our usual pace. There's a double whammy as our bodies ask for help to keep everything status quo.

A smoothie is another option if breakfast is not your thing or you don't want to deal with it. Find one that has enough protein and fat to keep you full. Just fruit or vegetables aren't going to work. I can vouch from experience on that one.

My morning smoothie consists of: banana, ice, milk, coffee, protein powder, and peanut butter. You might wrinkle your nose at it, but it has saved me because I am not a breakfast girl nor am I a milk girl. Yet this is enough to take off the edge of hunger that can lead to crankiness while also giving me the energy to get through the morning. It usually gives me about three hours until I'm hungry again. A fruit or vegetable smoothie would leave me hungry in an hour.

Look for smoothie recipes that have protein (like nuts, yogurt, tofu) in them. Or an omelet with cheese and vegetables.

For your other meals, you're looking for protein to bring you the energy to help your body cope. As I said before, it's okay to have the treats that you enjoy. Don't completely give up whatever you enjoy most. Instead make it a treat instead of something you have every night.

Make sure that whatever you're eating has taste and is something you like because you're more likely to want to eat it rather than taking one look at it and pushing it back in the refrigerator and grabbing a frozen pizza instead (or that ice cream).

There are a lot of great spices that can make greens and fish more exciting. We use a lot of chilies and spices especially for sautéed greens. Warming veggies makes them easier on the body to digest and they taste better than in a salad (and are better for you than in a dressing-laden salad).

Look online for recipes, especially for ones that you can make multiple meals at one time. This will help so you don't have to cook for several nights.

You hate cooking? Think of this as an investment in yourself. You could even take a cooking class– or two. It's a good way to meet people and learn something new about food. You may even find you like cooking; you just weren't sure how to do it for only yourself rather than at least two people or a large family.

Snacks are really important, too, and this is where it's crucial that you do something about the chips and the ice cream. I know that when you're hungry they're easy to reach for. Don't! Fill your refrigerator and pantry with protein-filled snacks. You want veggies that are easy to snack on– carrots, sugar snap peas, celery, etc. And something to dip them in (where you get the protein and fat because the vegetables are mostly just water and fiber) like Greek yogurt with dill or other spices. Hummus works well, too.

Other snacks include peanut butter on whole grain crackers (or rice crackers) or if you prefer something sweet, maybe apples to dip in peanut butter. Nuts are a good snack at any time.

There are many more ideas but these should get you started.

Journal

Are you taking good physical care of yourself? Why or why not? How can you do better?

Activity

Add a physical activity to your daily routine. And make one change a week in how you eat: whether it be cutting out junk food or adding breakfast. Return here after a week and write about how it went and what worked, what didn't, and how you can change it to make it work.

Chapter 39
Your Emotional Self

The emotional self might seem like the most logical piece of your holistic self to take care of, but it's very easy to neglect it. And often we do that because we are busy taking care of others, especially in certain relationships in our lives. We have children who need us, spouses whose lives we manage, family that wants us, friends who rely on us, and work that makes us think we have work harder or we might lose our jobs.

And in this we end up depleted and exhausted in a chair or a couch by the evening– or crawling up to bed knowing we didn't get the laundry or dishes done.

Then the next day we start over and do it again.

If we don't take the time to take care of ourselves and our emotional needs we find we become angry, short with others, depressed, and a whole host of other negative emotions and feelings.

I don't care how busy you are, you have take time for yourself or it will take its toll. And if you don't take care of yourself emotionally, it will manifest itself somehow and usually as a physical illness. If you find you always have a cold or you always feel run down, it's because you need to take a break and take care of your emotional side.

This means you might have to say no. The reality is that we can't do everything we want to in our lives. If we try to, some ball always will get dropped. Take a step back and find time for yourself. While you'll be reading about how to nourish your spiritual side, reflect here about the ways you can nourish your emotional self.

Do you take the time to read a book or a magazine? Or how about a hot bath with no one asking you for anything for thirty minutes (or more!)? A manicure? Spending time cooking a good dinner rather than rushing through ingredients in the refrigerator or finding something frozen that you can throw in the oven? Anything physical mentioned before, like going for a walk, could help you emotionally de-stress. Being out in the sunshine and letting it soak into you is a way of emotionally taking care of yourself as well.

And so is finding an outlet for your feelings– the challenging emotions. As all these aspects cross over into all the pieces that make up who we are, taking the time for an activity or hobby is a good way to let our minds rest. I took up painting about a year ago and it has helped me a lot during stressful times. I try to devote time each weekend to it. While it's hard to get started sometimes, to relax enough that I take my time rather than rush through it, I like that I'm being creative in a different way other than by writing.

Find people to spend time with whom you can share your concerns. I talked about connecting with others earlier and this is a good time for a reminder. Having someone to tell how you're feeling can be helpful. You might see a therapist or you just need someone to talk occasionally. Schedule lunch— something out of your routine— or a coffee. I believe that many times we simply need someone to listen where that person is able to hear us and offer what they get from what we're saying or spin it in a different way.

It might seem like a lot of parts of this book overlap each other because they do. But the hope is that the more times you read the messages, the more likely you are to follow through and make change, especially when you see how each one can help your life.

Journal

What are you doing to take care of your emotional self? What can you do better?

Chapter 40
Your Spiritual Self

For some people, this might be the hardest part of the book. I made sure I was clear before you got too far into this book that you would need to make a commitment to your spiritual self. I didn't make this up because I'm a person who runs around telling everyone to believe in God. Quite honestly, I'm the opposite– I spent a good part of my life battling the concept of God. However, once I realized how much better my life could be when I had a place to put my worries and my hopes, I was so much better off. However, this isn't the concept of God I was taught growing up which is why it took me longer to arrive at that part of the journey.

It was then that I also realized how much we have to balance all four pieces of us and if we only take care of one or two sides, we won't become who we are truly supposed to be.

If going to church is not your thing, I don't expect you to run out and start going now. What I'm asking instead is that you take the time to devote to prayer or meditation. I believe that they are almost one in the same, but people use different words depending on what works for them.

The first place to begin is finding a time to pray each day. While this will be different for everyone, I recommend carving out five minutes each morning. This may mean you wake up five minutes earlier, but you'll find it's worth it because it's a good way to center yourself and make it easier for you to cope with anything that's handed to you in the day ahead.

There are other times to put prayer into your life: you could pray while you're sitting at a red light or while you're waiting in the checkout lane of the grocery store. Think of how much time daily you find yourself waiting. These are great times to pray. Even just to say a simple thank you for that great parking spot you found or the fact that the sun is warming your skin.

But you also should find time for a longer prayer. For some people, first thing in the morning might not work. I pray while I'm run-walking my dogs Chaco and Hattie. I used to pray before I went to sleep at night, but usually I fell asleep and never finished the prayer (although if you're having issues falling asleep this isn't a bad way to get to sleep) and I have also prayed in the shower because I know that no one will bother me there– I won't hear the phone ring and usually no one is coming to talk to me. It might take a few tries to find what works for you.

The point is not to give up because this might feel fake to you when you begin. It might feel contrived, like you're forcing yourself to do something that doesn't feel comfortable.

And it might feel empty.

Remember, often things we do don't feel uncomfortable in the beginning. They might feel awkward or we might sneak around a corner so no one can see us praying because we don't feel like we really know what we're doing.

It's okay.

This is all about learning something new. What we don't often realize, despite the fact that we probably have been encouraged to pray our entire lives, no one has really taught us how to do it. Sure, we have been taught prayers but who has suggested ways to talk to God?

It's not that there is any particular way that we have to do it, because while I'm going to tell you what works for me, my hope is that in time you'll mold it into what works for you. That too is all about being your authentic self: you take something and you mold it into something that is about you. I simply give you the clay and a starting point.

Set up a place where you feel comfortable praying. I suggest you don't lie down or you might fall asleep. I wanted to pray by my pool and after a few times of sitting on the pool deck, I realized why people have prayer mats: the concrete was a little uncomfortable. While my major prayer for the day is done on my run-walk with my dogs, I sometimes pray at my desk before I begin working in the morning.

If you have space in your house to set up a place where you can always pray, that would work well. But don't be afraid to be flexible or move things around. It's not about where you pray, it's about where you feel comfortable praying. And if that's your kitchen table, then do it there.

Lighting a candle, a candle that you have specifically for your prayers, is part of designating space. That candle will become part of your prayer. I personally like to hold a rosary sometimes when I pray as well.

But then what do you do when you pray?

Don't be afraid to say what you feel! While I have admitted to not being a very prayerful person for a lot of my life, I never understood why people were afraid to tell God when they were angry. After all, that's why he's there. He's there to listen. He might not give us what we want or in the time frame we want it, but as we travel through our lives and if we choose to be aware, we will understand why events and situations in our lives roll out the way they do.

Be thankful for what you have. That's the best place to start. I go through the previous day and list all of what I am thankful for. When something challenging has happened, I try to be thankful for it but I admit it's hard. Instead, I find it's better for me to ask what I can learn from it especially so I can move on from it and then it's less likely to happen again.

We have talked before about being grateful and here's one major time in your day where you can list all that you are grateful for. Just because you were thankful for that parking spot yesterday doesn't mean you don't have to be again. The more thankful you are, the better you feel, especially about the small aspects in life.

After you have told God all that you're thankful for, then ask for what you want. Do you need help with something? You don't even have to ask for help, you can say, "I'm scared. I don't know what to do. Please help me." If you're feeing down, ask for more meaning in your life. Having meaning often brings us peace.

Often when we pray– and this is a good reason to pray– we feel as if we are standing in a room with all the doors closed or in the woods and we don't know where the path left off because it feels like the road less traveled.

I have a long list I ask for each day– strength, help, coping, letting go, moving forward. All sorts of things. And some goals I want to accomplish in the future. Many times I ask for help as I work through a challenge. If you have a big event coming up: divorce hearing, selling a house (or buying a house), a health concern, ask God to help you through it.

For me, giving it to God helps me worry less about it. I always remember the prayer for St. Theresa of Avila that says that all challenges are passing and that we have nothing to fear if we have God because somehow everything will work out.

The more I believe that, the more experiences I have of letting go, I then realize how right that is. I also have realized how much energy we waste on worry. We worry endlessly and then when everything works out, we look back and see that we didn't need to worry. Let God take care of it and we find we're not just more productive, but we feel free of those hovering black clouds that don't need to be there.

You don't have to ask for help in challenges either though. Maybe you have something you want to accomplish, something that feels impossible to you. Then ask God to help you with it. Maybe you want to accomplish something and you aren't sure how to do it. Then ask God for help with it– ask him to show you the way, roll out the carpet in front of you on how to make it happen. The more you ask, the more doors will open, ones you had no idea were there.

Finally– and this is the hardest part– listen.

We shouldn't talk the entire prayer. While we might have a lot to say, it's essential that we take at least a few moments to listen.

If we want help, then we need to hear what God has to say. You might get used to talking during your prayer so this is the part that might be harder because it will feel empty a lot of the time.

That doesn't mean that nothing is happening. Think how many times we are in a conversation, especially one where someone is in a lot of pain, and they stop talking. What do we do? We keep talking. Sometimes though we need to give that person a chance to think for a moment, for them to hear themselves in the empty space of the conversation because often that's where they get their answers.

It's the same in prayer. After all, God can't speak to you if you keep talking. He's not going to talk over you. He needs you to be quiet and let him speak in his way. While the space might feel empty and even when you close out the prayer it will still feel empty, you never know when the answer will come. It might come during the prayer or it might come two weeks later. A thought might pop into your head and it's the answer. If you gave it to God, you gave him a chance to speak to you. That sets everything in motion.

Think of prayer as a chance to sit with God in conversation— or with Jesus. While some people say they have different voices, I have just started to understand that. For me, I have a vision of what I think Jesus is like and because of what a priest suggested to me once, often Jesus and I go surfing. Or we sit on the beach together and talk.

I understand the challenge of this though. When I was a kid, I remember how I would set up something with my Barbies to play with (like a scene— my younger sister and my best friend used to build elaborate houses with boxes and carpet samples). I would spend a whole lot of time on it. And when it was finished, when it was time to actually play out the scene? I didn't want to play anymore.

This is my challenge with surfing with Jesus: we're out there on the ocean or our surfboards or we're sitting on the beach in our wetsuits, our surfboards off to the side, and then what?

Nothing.

This is not Jesus' fault. I know we're having a conversation but I'm the one who is struggling because I've set the scene and suddenly when it comes to the rest part, I can't relax long enough to be present. And listen.

We live in a world where we are constantly moving; we always have something to do. When we finally sit down or go to bed, we can't sleep because we can't stop our minds from working. At the end of a long workday, sometimes I'll take my dog Hattie for a walk and I find I can't turn it off. I'll keep looking at my phone, using the excuse that the workday isn't over yet (it's usually around 3:00 in the afternoon). That's how we are in prayer: we can only hear if we turn it off, if we're present.

And often when we finally start to settle in, our minds begin to wander. We think about the laundry we need to do and the phone call we forgot to make. Suddenly we've wandered off away Jesus who is patiently waiting for us.

You change this with slow steps. Start by setting a timer for five minutes and use the first part of your prayer to be thankful for anything you can think of that you're grateful for right down to the sun shining and the fact that you can breathe without difficulty.

Once you finish that, go into the list of what you want. This isn't a Christmas list for Santa Claus of material items but the challenges you want help with, the goals you want to accomplish, the pain you want to move past. Whatever it is, this is the place to put it.

Then with whatever time is left (and there might not be much— maybe a minute) force yourself to sit there with Jesus. You don't have to say anything. Maybe you're just sitting together quietly watching the ocean waves lap on the shore or you're taking in the mountain view in front of you.

There is no need to feel uncomfortable in this situation. Jesus isn't the cute guy you just met at the coffee shop or tripped over his cart in the grocery store. He's an old friend you've known all your life and you're picking up your friendship wherever you left off. You should feel comfortable with him, even in the silence.

When the timer goes off, you'll feel like five minutes have flown by. You might even realize you need more than five minutes. Do this every day and add more time if you need to. Gradually work up to having a conversation with Jesus. You can even tell him about the phone call you forgot to make or how much you hate to do laundry. It's a place to start and let him respond to you. If you find yourself drifting away, that's a good time to bring yourself back by telling him what you're drifting away about (probably the laundry).

This will not come easy to you and that's okay. We've been taught that prayer should be easy and, yes, it's easy to recite a bunch of words strewn together and that's important. But just like in life, we've never spent enough time cultivating our listening skills. As you do this with Jesus, you'll find it changing in your life, too.

Recently, I've added Our Lady of Guadalupe (whose feast day falls on my birthday) and Saint Rita (the saint of the impossible) to my prayer. I picture the four of us (Jesus included) sitting around a table in a kitchen. I have my laptop in front of me and they each have a cup of coffee or tea in front of them. We're having a conversation about my writing and I'm telling them what I need help with. Many mornings though, I am unable to sit down in my vision of the prayer and I'm pacing the kitchen where we're located because that's how I usually feel. They watch me patiently and I finally slip into my chair and then we're all staring at each other. I'm working to listen better though.

Where you need to be with God is where you feel at peace. For me that's on my surfboard and it's also while I'm out run-walking my dogs. Think about a place that feels peaceful, calm, and happy and that's where you should meet God. It's a place where you feel comfortable talking with him and feel like you can listen to him there. But the kitchen is good, too.

Finally, once I heard we should be "courageous in prayer." There is nothing to fear. I have also heard we should "just ask." As I said before, you might not always get what you want in the time frame you want it in but if you're aware, you'll notice the changes inside you and around you.

Nourishing your spiritual self isn't just about prayer for everyone though.

Going to church is one way that people cultivate their spirituality. They do this because they need that hour or so in a place where they can rest, where they put aside the rest of life, and focus on God. Have you ever left church feeling worse than when you came? I'm guessing probably not (unless the clergy upset you with a sermon). We usually feel better from the music and also from the community.

Think back on the television show "Little House on the Prairie." Going to church on Sunday was also about getting together with community. It was the one time where people gathered together because they made Sundays a day of rest. That's why people gather after church for pancakes or coffee and doughnuts (in the case of those of us in New Mexico, breakfast burritos). When we nourish our spiritual selves, we do it by connecting with others.

There are always volunteer opportunities within a church or groups to be a part of. These help us connect with like-minded people while also giving back. And if have a church that we enjoy attending, we'll want to give back somehow to make sure that the church stays running.

Journal

What are you doing to take care of your spiritual self? What can you do better?

Chapter 41
The Intellectual Self

We don't often include this part of ourselves when we think of our holistic selves. But what we forget is that this is yet another piece of us that needs nurturing. We can feel when we're not getting enough of something: it's like the spiritual hunger than I mentioned before. We crave what we're not getting.

Taking care of ourselves intellectually can mean reading more often– and picking up books that are more challenging than reading Harry Potter. Reading Harry Potter isn't bad and it's at least reading, but if we want to grow we need books that are going to force us to think. In some ways, this book should be intellectually challenging because I'm constantly asking you to do something (although what I'm asking you to do is usually about more than nurturing your intellect).

Taking a class is intellectually stimulating. What do you want to know more about? What are your interests? Or going to a museum. Crossword puzzles. Doing things that force you to think.

While you might have a job that is very intellectually stimulating and you're thinking, "I think all day. That's the last thing I want to do when I get home." But there you're doing something for your work: at home you're doing it for you. Find a few minutes to at least do a word search.

But it's even better when you can make it a social opportunity, too. For instance, there are book clubs that aren't just about a group of women getting together to drink wine and be away from their families. Some of them actually want to discuss the book and bounce what they learned or questioned on others.

Journal
How have you taken care of yourself intellectually? What has worked? What hasn't?

Activity
Put one intellectual activity in place in your life this week and return here to write about it. Did it work? If not, try something else. If it did, keep at it. Return and write about your experiences until you find something that works for you and you feel confident you can keep going.

Flowers by Day, Stars by Night: Finding Happiness after Loss and Change

Chapter 42
Setting Goals

Without realizing it, you've probably already set some goals particularly in the previous section. If not, take the time to set a goal for each of the sections we just talked about: emotional, physical, spiritual, and intellectual. This is not an optional activity in this book– it's a requirement for graduation!

If you have never set goals before, think about what you want to accomplish to make you be better, go forward, be who you want to be. Also, think about smaller goals that will help you accomplish the big goal.

For instance, if your goal is to lose ten pounds, how will you do it? What kind of exercise will you do and how often? How will you change your eating?

It's important to have smaller goals to meet along the way because you won't (contrary to some of the commercials on television) lose ten pounds in a week. You want to have rewards (we'll be talking about those shortly) as well to keep you motivated.

After you have come up with your smaller goals for each area, then write your main goals on one piece of paper and hang it somewhere that you can see it. This could be on your refrigerator or your bathroom mirror. It has to be some place where you will see it and be reminded of it. You don't want to forget what you're trying to accomplish especially when life tries to throw you off track– or you try to throw you off track.

Then share with a trust family member or friend your goals, people who will support you and not try to sabotage you. If you don't have anyone like that in your life you will need to be strong and not let him or her get to you. The positive, supportive people will be there, acting as cheerleaders, walking with you as you work toward your goals.

Journal

What are your four goals and the smaller supporting goals that will help you achieve them?

Flowers by Day, Stars by Night: Finding Happiness after Loss and Change

Chapter 43
The Rewards

You should always have something in place to reward yourself. This doesn't have to be anything big, just a little boost to keep you working toward your big goal. You also can have small rewards plus a big reward for when you complete the major goal. Mostly these are to keep you motivated because you know from the past that it's easy to not complete a goal. Having something in place helps to ensure you will get there.

I started my writing rewards several years ago. Writing is really important to me, but I felt like I wasn't making the time for it and letting everything else get in the way. I needed to take the time to write daily, but I need a little extra boost to get it done. My goal each month was to write fifty pages on a manuscript.

During the month I would come up with a reward. It wasn't like I went to the mall and purposely sought out something for the reward; usually it was because I stumbled on something. There were months where I didn't have a reward until I was almost done writing for the month. It didn't matter because the point was that I found something that got me excited, especially as I got near the end of my pages and maybe I was distracted or didn't think I could finish.

All I had to do was think of the item in the bag waiting for me and realize that I couldn't stop writing. Many months it was dresses, once it was a milkshake machine. Sometimes it has been Kate Spade purses. One big month it was a Roomba robot vacuum cleaner that meant I didn't have to vacuum the dog fur every morning. But I had to earn it! For me, these are items that I never would have bought without "earning" them, but I felt I could justify them this way. And in the process I was doing what I want most: to write books.

Your rewards might be totally different. Maybe getting a manicure or pedicure is something you feel you could justify if you lost those five pounds this month. You also can use food as a reward. I do not believe that any person should deny herself anything for the rest of her life unless it is a health issue. If you want to have a strawberry sundae after you've lost five pounds, it's not going to kill you. Now if you have several after you lost five pounds that might be different. Having a sundae as a treat is a good way to reward yourself and also keep you from bingeing on sundaes later.

Each person's treat should be unique. It should be something that when you think about it, it helps you stay the course to keep your goals in mind. And it will be like a mini goal along the way. "If I lose five of the twenty pounds I want to lose, I'm going to buy a new pair of jeans."

You might even get a new clothing item that you know you will fit into as you lose the weight.

Or you could reward yourself by putting money aside for a trip. Each time you meet your goal, you put something in a bank account for it. Or maybe there is something you've wanted to buy like a purse or piece of jewelry.

And if you can't think of something, ask some friends if they have ideas for you. It might even turn into a fun game for all of you and they might want to support you even more by holding your carrot (the reward) in front of you when you say you don't want to work out that day.

Journal

What are your rewards for completing your goals?

Chapter 44
The 50 Goals

While you're trying out new activities or immersing yourself in hobbies you haven't put time into for many years, start a new page in your journal for 50 goals.

There are a few lessons I learned from Steve Mazzarella in his health class my sophomore year of high school. These lessons I have used when I was a classroom teacher and also with my groups of separated and divorced women.

The first one is the 50 goals. Mazz, as we called him, had us write out 50 goals. It could be anything we wanted to accomplish in our lives, no matter how big or small it seemed. To this day I have no idea what happened to my list because I would love to see how much of it I accomplished. Something I learned along the way is that by putting something on paper is like throwing it out to the universe, essentially you're saying, "Hey, I want to accomplish this." And when you do that, it's more likely to happen.

It might seem daunting to write out 50 goals, but they can be as small as seeing a movie you've always wanted to see or as big as surfing in Fiji (oops, sorry, that would be on my list). And you don't have to do the list all at once. Start it and when you're exercising, washing dishes, standing in a long checkout line at the grocery store, or folding laundry, let your mind wander about some of the goals you would like to accomplish. But don't forget about it! My suggestion is that your goal– as in your goal for the 50 goals– is to finish it by the time you have completed this book.

Journal

What are your 50 goals?

Flowers by Day, Stars by Night: Finding Happiness after Loss and Change

Chapter 45
The Collage

When you're working on your 50 goals, you also should create a collage that will motivate you. You can use old magazines or you can draw something– whatever works for you. This also might be a good time to gather a few supportive friends together and the group of you can work on collages together. It always helps to have several people because the art supplies multiply and make it more fun to have more to work with.

As I mentioned earlier, when I was in high school– maybe even junior high– I used to create collages out, mostly out of magazines. My sister was working on a computer science degree at the time and would bring home reams of green and white striped paper– the dot matrix kind that could be torn apart– and I would take about four or five or them and leave them connected to make one big collage of words, phrases, quotes, pictures, or whatever I found inspirational from magazines.

When you're done with the collage, place it somewhere that you can see it often. You will be creating several items that you'll need to hang and it might be good to put them in different places. Something could go on the bathroom mirror, something else on the refrigerator door (tape will work on a stainless refrigerator where magnets won't).

You might even create several themes. Each one could have a theme: one for weight loss, another for goals you want to accomplish. And yet another of what seems like impossible dreams to come true. Or you could have one of anything that inspires you just to have something to focus on when you don't feel that great.

While writing is good, it also helps to have something visual to see and the collages make for that added impact.

Flowers by Day, Stars by Night: Finding Happiness after Loss and Change

Chapter 46
Self Care

I realize there are a lot of moving parts to going forward in your life. What you'll find is that some aspects of this book will be more important than others each day. As you work through everything, you'll feel that certain pieces register with you more than others. You also might find in the weeks or months ahead, as everything changes, that you need to reach for this guide because something that didn't mean something to you at the time does now.

It's okay because that means you're making progress. You had something to work on at one point, but as you process through it, you had room to take on something else.

But there is something really important not to forget: taking care of yourself.

We don't have anyone to take care of us so we need to make sure that we always put ourselves first. I know it's hard when you have a life filled with demands, but if you're feeling rundown or exhausted, that's not going to change unless you do something about it.

Think about the activities that help you regain your balance in the world. These are going to be different for each person, but here some suggestions below. And you will find we've discussed many of them before, but I believe they are important enough to repeat.

For some people, going to church is a good way to rest and also give oneself some spiritual time. For others, going for a walk is helpful– being outside in the sunshine or the elements (one can enjoy a walk in the snow). And for others, it's sitting still: maybe in a hot bath, reading a book or magazine, or working on a knitting project.

As my life has changed, painting has become a way for me to relax while creating something. I have found that I need to take some time each weekend for myself or I'm not ready to go for a new week when Monday arrives. Cooking also helps. While some people need the kind of relaxation where they veg out in front of the television, mine is more about creativity.

I like activities where I can instantly create something (a book takes a while to come together!) like watching the colors go on a canvas or making a meal or desert. The added benefit of cooking and baking is there is an element of doing something for others as well. I like the challenge of making healthy, but tasty meals and desserts and then sharing them with others.

But having a weekend to simply rest can be good, too.

Remember, none of what you're doing is easy. I will never say it is. I do know it's worth it, but I also know you need to take time for yourself. Working through so much pain, loss, fear, anger, disappointment, and everything else takes energy. Plus your life isn't stopping just because you're working on this book. It's an added piece of an already full life.

Allow yourself treats. Have that favorite chocolate sometimes. Get a manicure. Indulge in a movie while you're in your pajamas on a Friday night. Do the things that nourish you.

Journal

What nourishes you? Make a list of activities that you can reach for when you feel exhausted and need to replenish yourself. Be sure these are handy so when you're laying on the couch and want to do something to take care of yourself, you can look at the list. Often when we are exhausted, we don't have the energy to think. The list is prevention: having it there for you when you need it.

Chapter 47
The Check In

You've been thinking, talking about, and writing about a lot of stuff. I say "stuff" because there is a lot here. Part of you might feel empowered and excited because you know that while this isn't easy, you want to see life on the other side of the mountain: the ocean, the green valley, whatever you envision your happy place to be.

Another part of you might be scared. This is real, this hurts, this means facing difficult places in your life.

And yet another part of you (I doubt all of you because you probably wouldn't be reading this far into the book) is in denial.

I know this feeling and that's why I wrote about it at the beginning.

I can still remember sitting in the sand on my beach towel at Huntington Beach on a late May morning two years ago and reading a book about finding "the one." I could see where I had done a lot of what the book suggested, but I reached a point where the book annoyed me because it was something I didn't want to face about myself. Really, it was about letting go of someone in my life who was actually causing a lot of emotional havoc. Obviously I wasn't ready to let go.

I wasn't angry at the book, I just didn't agree with that part. It wasn't until several months later that when I finally acknowledged I needed to let go, that I realized the book was right. I had to get rid of this person and once I did, my husband came into my life.

If you're annoyed at the book (or probably me for suggesting you deal with something) then it means you aren't going to truly move forward until you remove that wall and take care of whatever is behind it. I have seen people in life coaching who are obviously not ready to change (despite what they say) because everything I suggest is responded with "I did that but it didn't work." The bricks get piled higher and higher with each statement that comes out of someone's mouth.

So if you find yourself fighting the book, take a step back and reflect on exactly what it is that you're pushing back against. If you're having a hard time identifying it, then ask a friend to help you. But I'm guessing you know exactly what it is, it's more that it's easier– no comfortable– to remain where you're at.

But do you really want to stay there? Sure it's comfortable, like that pair of worn out pajamas that you keep wearing because they are soft, but they're falling apart. You wouldn't dare be seen in public in them and your family makes fun of you each time you put them on.

You don't want to stay there. So go back to the chapter or place that you're resisting and challenge yourself to work through it. Think of a good reward for yourself after you finish at least doing the lesson I've suggested. You might not get it perfectly the first time especially if you've been pushing back on it– it will probably take several tries– but reward yourself for stepping into unknown territory.

As you continue to work through *Flowers by Day, Stars by Night*, you'll see the difference in how you feel. Being comfortable is overrated. I don't believe that we always should be stepping out of our boxes nor do I believe we always have to suffer to experience happiness, but by making these strides forward into uncharted territory you'll experience happiness and accomplishment as you never have before.

Journal

What are you doing to take care of yourself?

Chapter 48
The Rearview Mirror

While I have harped on the importance of not spending your time looking back because you can't change the past, as we draw to a close I hope you will spend some time reflecting on how far you have come during this process. I am assuming that you've done all the journals and activities, I know that by completing them (and doing them with your whole heart rather than with no emotion), you have accomplished something.

We often can't see what we have learned from something when we're in the thick of it. I often tell people, "Even thought I can see how you've changed, I know you don't see it. But as you move further away from it, it will become more obvious what's in the rearview mirror."

As I said in the beginning, it's not about the destination. Life is always going to have its up and downs and challenges, it's how we react to them. This journey will never end because we are always called to reach deeper into ourselves to learn more. If we take this opportunity to learn what we are supposed to from it, it won't repeat itself and we will be open to new learning experiences as we continue to grow. And while there might be other challenges ahead, we will find we are stronger and ready to face them. We know what tools we have in the tool kit and we'll know what to do when it feels overwhelming and too challenging. We'll come up against it and it won't knock us down.

Journal

Looking back on reading your work and completing the activities, what have you learned? What have you accomplished?

Flowers by Day, Stars by Night: Finding Happiness after Loss and Change

Chapter 49
Finding your Authentic Self

While I believe that I never really strayed from being my authentic self, I think that some parts of it got put into piles while I did other things. This is particularly true of my writing. It was something I always wanted to do, but there was always that reality that I had to work to pay the bills. After all, I don't have a money tree in my backyard and I prefer to live in a house rather than a tent.

It was easier to take the time for my writing before I got married because I had more time for it. But after I was married, I spent a lot of time on my then-husband's business. He was in sales and it was important I do my part. I thought that if I did, eventually I would get time back for myself.

And to some extent I did because once things were moving along fairly well, I backed off and put myself into finishing my book for sibling survivors of suicide.

I am very grateful for everything that came after that: I have been around the world speaking and talking to people about loss and finding hope. But in that process and my then-husband's head injury, so much of me got covered up and pushed aside as I tried to keep everything together.

While I never set out to save the world, I gave a lot of my time to others. It might have looked like I was doing a lot for me, but really I was doing more for others, believing I had a job to do to help everyone else. And I did self care– I ran, I had my pool, my dogs, dinner parties.

But there was so much I didn't do and when I realized I didn't want to put my fiction off any longer, that was the start of the new road to realizing I needed to take more time for me. By then I also was realizing I had done what I felt I needed to do for the suicidology field.

By the time I divorced and moved back to Illinois, I had more time on my hands, but it took me a while to mold and form my new life. I began to write more consistently. However, once that was in place, I saw that I wanted to do things that didn't involve sitting in front of my computer.

First I took up golf, a suggestion from my neighbor who thought I could meet a man that way (it didn't work although my husband and I do both like to golf and it's something we do together). Then I added tennis. My mom laughed at me one day and asked if I was going to add kayaking to my activities (it never occurred to me!).

In all this though, there was something I had been neglecting: my creative self.

I had been a kid who loved to draw and we always had a lot of crayons, markers, and paper around. As I got older, I began to sew, mostly making Barbie clothes with my younger sister and eventually quilts. I was kind of bored with that (although I still have a lot of fabric I should make into things). And I had wanted to do tile mosaics, but that also hasn't worked out yet.

So I decided to take up painting.

It took me a while to get started. I think I was afraid to. But finally I realized the paintings didn't have to be perfect. Plus I had to accept that they wouldn't always work as they did in my head (much like writing). It's the perfectionist in me that has a hard time letting that go.

And I had to remember that a lot of it is not about the finished product so much is that it's about the journey. But painting was easier in many ways: it takes up less space than quilting and it's something I can do while the television is on or outside by the pool in the cool hours of a summer morning.

Mostly though, as I started to create more paintings, I saw a side of me come out that I had been there all along, but I didn't have a place to put. I saw my retro modern style and the bright and bold colors that I love. And I was filling my walls with colors and things or scenes that made me happy. It felt like me.

I know that you're going through a painful time. I know that it's not what you asked for. But I also know that you can't turn the clock back. We can look back all we want and think about how much we wished things were different. But it's not worth putting your energy there or trying to figure out what went wrong, what you did wrong, what you wish you could do differently if you could go back in time.

You're wasting energy doing all of that. Instead, look up and look ahead. Somewhere over there, where you probably can't see, is the sun shining bright. It's whatever you want to be: a mountain scene, an ocean scene. Or maybe both!

And if I had to guess, what you see now isn't complete darkness. Ahead of you there is some light at the horizon, not much but there is some. It's just like the ember of hope that burns inside you. I know some of you won't even look up to see that light— you're still too busy looking behind you at what is over. And others of you are looking down because you're afraid to look ahead.

Chapter 50
Finding your Authentic Self Part II

Some of you may think that you don't know who you are and that's making it a challenge to complete the tasks I'm asking you to do. You really do know who you are, you just aren't as aware of it as you think you are.

I have always known who I wanted to be. From the time I was six years old, I knew I wanted to be an author. Not just a writer but a fiction writer. My first story was told on a piece of Holiday Inn hotel stationery where I had drawn a picture and had my mom write out what was going on. When I could start to draw and write I made picture books. My younger sister Denise and I spent a lot of our time creating stories around our Raggedy Anns and Barbies.

There were some detours along the way. In junior high and high school, right up until the time I was choosing a college, I thought about becoming a disc jockey and entering broadcast journalism. And in other years I floated the idea of becoming a psychologist or an athletic trainer.

It was in junior high that someone told me I would need to support myself because I would not be making money right away as a novelist and that's when I started to work toward a career in journalism.

However, after my sister's death when I was in college, my life took a turn because I felt like there was something else I needed to do. And for about fifteen years I produced several books related to coping with suicide loss and spoke around the world about the topic.

I tell you this because while I didn't realize it at the time, I still was the same person deep inside me: I was still the girl who wanted to be a writer. And when I woke up to that reminder, as if someone posted it on my refrigerator for me to see, I began the journey toward spending more time on my writing.

Life may have taken you places you didn't plan– or didn't want to go– but because you can't go back and change the past, don't keep fighting what has happened to you. Be grateful for it because I'm sure there are aspects of it you can pull out and use in your life today.

I can easily look back on my life and be annoyed that I devoted so much time to helping others when I should have been doing things for me– for my writing– and that there was a marriage that didn't work out. It would be easy to get irritated and feel like too much life has passed me by and I've missed out on something.

What I know is all those experiences have helped make me a stronger person— and write. It's like people have been walking this journey with me and the more they tell me, the more I learn. Traveling has opened me up to worlds to write about and scenes to set. My first marriage gave me opportunities I don't think I would have had otherwise. Without all of this happening to me, I would not be who I am or where I am today.

And in this I also can look back and see how much my intuition is part of my authentic self. Several years ago, when I was single, I had multiple people egging me on to do the online dating gig. One person said I needed to date "anyone and everyone" even if I didn't see a future with that person. I realize people were trying to be helpful, especially if they were in secure relationships and want everyone else around them to be in one, but this wasn't me.

I started a profile on an online site and never finished it because it didn't feel right. The more I filled out, the more it felt wrong.

While I had a life that got me out (even though I was working at home) and around people, I just couldn't seem to find someone to date

So I signed up with a local matchmaker.

I won't reveal the details, but while it wasn't a disaster it was pretty close. Mostly it was a waste of my time and energy. It felt totally wrong to me, but I knew it would get people off my back so I did it and went on two dates. After that, I canceled out.

I don't agree with online dating or matchmaking (not the kind that friends do as that's how I met my husband) because I believe that you will meet someone in the course of your daily activities or by getting out, not by having someone who doesn't really know you or who thinks she has a formula to set you up.

I realize that some people are comfortable with this, but it feels fake because someone is judging you on a photo and a paragraph you have written about yourself, not laughing with you when you knocked all the oranges off the pyramid at the grocery store.

About two weeks after I canceled with the matchmaker, I met my husband.

There have been other times in my life where I have done something because I felt pressured to do it from others, yet to me it was wrong.

Let me add, there is a difference between feeling scared because something is wrong and because something is new.

You might have once been scared to go off the high dive into the swimming pool. The other kids, including your friends and your siblings, were egging you on. The key here is that you *wanted* to do it, you were just too scared and you used fear to make it look like you didn't want to do it. It didn't feel wrong, in fact, it looked like a lot of fun.

And guess what happened when you finally did it?

Of course, you got back in line and did it again.

If you haven't been off a high dive recently, or if you never did jump off one, I challenge you now to do it (if it's winter I'm sure you can find a local high school or YMCA pool with one). Don't let your fear get to you. Remind yourself why you are there. And after you've done it, you'll be splashing around and laughing. You will feel healing going off the high dive and with that comes strength that is your springboard to your future.

However, if swimming isn't your thing, I'm sure there is another activity you can do that will bring the same result.

The point is that in our authentic selves, there is a difference between what feels right and what feels wrong. Each time you're faced with a new situation, take a step back and examine the activity. If it's something you really want to do, you're just scared, then do it. But if it's truly something that feels wrong, then walk away and find something that you would rather do.

Flowers by Day, Stars by Night: Finding Happiness after Loss and Change

Chapter 51
Ditch the fear

You can have what you want ahead of you as soon as you decide you want it. You've gotten this far in this book why do you want to give up now?

I always think back to a friend who asked me once when I was going through my divorce how I thought I would be in the future. At first I said fine and then I said, "No, great."

You're not going to be fine. You're going to be great.

Flowers by Day, Stars by Night: Finding Happiness after Loss and Change

Chapter 52
Filling the Empty Spaces

Friday nights were the worst. My Friday routine took me to the store to prep for the weekend. I shopped at my local grocery store, Sam's Club, and then Target. I would plan our dinners, which usually included steak fajitas, on Saturday night.

And when I divorced suddenly I had nothing to do on Friday nights. This became the first obviously empty space in my life, one that I had a hard time filling, but I worked diligently at. I didn't turn down Friday night invitations with friends and their families. And when I moved back to Albuquerque I went to the driving range around dinnertime on Friday night just so I didn't have to be at home.

Coming back to Albuquerque was easier because I had friends who were happy to bring their kids over to swim in my pool. I filled my weekends with a group of friends: we would have "lunch and a swim" on whatever day worked around soccer and other activities.

Having friends over made me feel less like my life wasn't the same and it was part of forcing myself to go forward, to make out a life, although a different one.

In Illinois it was harder, but I devoted more time to my running. I started to go to daily mass before I would start work. And I walked Chaco and Gidget– the two dogs that went with me in the move– every afternoon. My neighbor taught me to knit. I spent more time creating new recipes.

I did whatever I could that made me happy even though inside I missed the routine I'd once had. Now that I reflect back, what I see is that I forced myself on a road although not knowing where it would lead. I had learned enough in my past to do things even if they were activities that wouldn't stick forever. It was like I was trudging forward in the snow when I couldn't see the ground.

The point was I tried to fill the empty spaces with things for me. I also took on a freelance gig with the local newspaper. I did anything I could to meet more people. I dressed nicely when I went out, even just to the grocery store. I wanted to feel good and I feel good when I know I look good.

But I won't say it was easy because I hated that my future was unknown. Still, I accepted that this was where I was supposed to be at the time and I made the most of that time to do things for me.

Filling the empty spaces shouldn't be hard. While it might not feel natural because you're used to the routine you once had that no longer exists, the key is that you do something.

It's true that keeping busy is helpful. While there is a point where someone can be too busy and that's not helpful, having activities and events to look forward to will keep one's mind off what one doesn't have.

You've been making goals, but in those goals you also should be thinking about activities and hobbies you've put aside. If you can't think of any, walk around your house and look into closets for anything you might have wanted to do but put away and forgot about. Talk to friends and family and ask about what you might have mentioned in the past. But my guess is that you have something maybe you never told anyone you wanted to do.

Now's your chance. Nothing is impossible. It might seem that way but once you throw it out to the universe, you never know what will land in your lap, just as surfing did in my mine.

Chapter 53
Looking Back, Moving Forward

Whew. It's been quite a journey.

I hope that you really took your time with *Flowers by Day, Stars by Night*, that you didn't read it in a weekend and now it's Sunday evening and you're going to start another book tomorrow. While I don't believe this should have taken you more than a few weeks, my hope is that you took your time because some of the journal entries should have been done over a period of a few days. While you probably thought of things to write when you started, having time to think about it probably gave you more ideas.

This is not an easy journey and it's not one that many people are willing to take. Some people choose to remain in their pain. For some they do this because they think it's where they are supposed to be while others aren't sure how to get out of it. But you have picked up this guide because somewhere inside of you, you know that ember of hope is there and that you don't have to live in pain. You believe that your life could be better and the key is that you want it to be better. My guess is that your view of hope has changed along the journey of working through this book.

Maybe you aren't sure how to make it better and maybe you've started on this road many times, but you somehow find yourself going back to where you started and getting back on the old road.

I hope you were able to keep going this time, that you found what you were missing before. And maybe you aren't as far as you'd like to be on this journey, but you see that you're working on it and that you're making progress.

Don't give up!

Keep working on the lessons. Return to the parts of the book of the pieces that are especially challenging. Read them again. Do the journal entries again. Talk with someone you trust about these pieces.

I wrote *Flowers by Day, Stars by Night* because I want to help people have happy lives. I believe that despite what has happened to any of us, it still can happen. And I believe I have lessons to share of what has helped me.

It took me a long time to realize how much of what I did for myself would benefit others, but I also have learned that sometimes you have to travel far enough on your own road before you can use what you have learned to help others.

Flowers by Day, Stars by Night: Finding Happiness after Loss and Change

For me, one of the keys if something happens to me is asking what I can learn from it. How can I use it go forward? How can I use it to help others? I hate when I am faced with challenges but I have learned to accept them and work at learning from them. Once I do that, I feel peace that I can maneuver through them and I don't feel like I am sitting in darkness.

There are many doors you've had to close on this journey. You've lost some people you cared about along the way through a variety of circumstances. Some have died, some have walked away from you, and you have distanced yourself from others because of the pain they inflicted on you.

You might have also had to leave a house you loved or moved to another state. No matter what has happened to you, be assured that even though you feel like a bunch of doors have slammed shut on you and that you feel as if you are sitting in darkness, the darkness won't last forever. As you continue to go forward and strengthen yourself and work toward being your authentic self, the doors will begin to open.

They won't all fly open at once, but over this process you'll realize that some light is emerging into the room and then another light. And the light will get brighter. And suddenly all your hard work is paying off. It's just like weight loss: as you work at it by exercising and eating better, it won't happen overnight (after all, you didn't put this weight on overnight), but one day you'll stop and realize that not only do you feel better, but your clothes are too big. And you'll look in the mirror and see you're more confident and actually like the way you look.

The doors will open. You won't feel so afraid of the future, you'll embrace it and realize that those 50 goals are attainable. Hey, you might not be sure how, but you took a chance by writing them down. And I bet there have been other times since you started working on this book that miracles have happened in your life. I have a friend who once said that miracles are around us every day. Maybe not the big ones like someone being cured of fatal disease, but the kind where we find new opportunities and people landing in our laps. These are the result of our hard work.

Keep at it. No matter where you are now, don't give up. You have every opportunity in front of you if you choose to see the glass as half full. And if you are open to them. Half the battle as we talked about before is that self talk. Believe that you're capable of anything, but you have to take care of your part in this: you have to do your work to be the person you're supposed to be, to nourish all sides of yourself– emotional, physical, spiritual, and intellectual– and to make sure you live that authentic life.

When I announced I was going to Australia the last time, a friend made a comment that it was too far, that she would never go. It wasn't that she didn't want to go, she didn't think she could survive the long plane trip. A year later she found herself going to Europe and now is unstoppable with her foreign travel. I won't be surprised if she makes it to Australia one day. I know that I got to Australia— not once but three times— because as impossible as it seemed in my life, just by knowing that one day I wanted to go there, I threw it out to the universe. And guess what? It happened.

We should all dream big. But dream big only if you're willing to put the work into it. That's taking care of yourself and continuing to believe that the stars are endless in the sky. When I left Hong Kong the one time I was there I had someone who wanted to meet with me but we ran out of time.

"You never know when I'll be back," I told her. "I never say never."

Hong Kong might be a world away from the United States with the Pacific Ocean dividing us, but if life got me there once, I might get there again. I feel that way when I say goodbye to anyone. After so many losses in my life, for so long goodbyes were very painful because I worried that I would never see someone again. It always will happen that way, that's life. But I also know that we never know when we will see someone again.

Leave that door open, keeping the glass not just half full but overflowing, and on a challenging day, to tell yourself to "stay the course" and continue to forge forward with what you believe.

The results are down the road if you keep heading that way. And I'm on the side of the road cheering you on. I am not quite where I wanted to be, or where I thought I would be by this time in my life, but I understand it's not about the end result, it's about the journey and all that I have experienced along the way. After all, if I didn't experience all that I have, I wouldn't have anything to write about or share with others.

Whatever you truly want is there for you. Keep seeing the hope past the darkness and you too will get there.

Flowers by Day, Stars by Night: Finding Happiness after Loss and Change

Other Books by Michelle L. Rusk
The Green Dress

As Michelle Linn-Gust
Do They Have Bad Days in Heaven? Surviving the Suicide Loss of a Sibling
Ginger's Gift: Hope and Healing through Dog Companionship
Rocky Roads: The Journeys of Families through Suicide Grief
The Australian Pen Pal
Seeking Hope: Stories of the Suicide Bereaved
Sisters: The Karma Twist
A Winding Road: A Handbook for those Supporting the Suicide Bereaved
Conversations with the Water: A Memoir of Cultivating Hope

Flowers by Day, Stars by Night: Finding Happiness after Loss and Change

About the Cover and the Artist

Waya'aisiwa "Gary" Keene of Acoma Pueblo, New Mexico, drew and colored the cover with permanent ink. He is a self-taught artist with no formal training. His family comes from the Eagle clan.

According to Waya'aisiwa, on the cover, all the flowers are circles in the valley below the girl. All the solid black represents clouds and the brown is sunshine. The fine lines are rain and he has incorporated eagles and turtles into the design as well.

The stars can be male or female, whichever you choose.

The woman is pointing toward a bright star in the distance. What she's pointing at are all the hopes, dreams, and goals waiting for her. And you.